SHELTERED

IN THE

ROCK

By

Margaret Lattin

Margaret Lattin

Cover design by Hadassa Manchester

ISBN :9781518873928

This book is dedicated to our nine grandchildren who have enriched our lives with their diversified talents and personalities. Our prayer for them is that they may dwell in the Shelter of the Most High.

The three Lattins: Jael, Zachary and Benjamin

The two Thomas': Brandon and Jacob

The four Manchesters: Hadassa, Kezia, Sarai and Elie

ACKNOWLEGMENTS

Somewhere I read that: "There is no such thing as a self-made man, because all along the way someone has touched his life and helped him."

There are many who have helped me along the way to put my life-story into print. Although I had written the first part when we first returned from the mission field, it lay hidden until my two granddaughters, Hadassa and Kezia, twisted my arm to join them at a writer's club in Temecula. I dusted off the manuscript and brought several pages to be critiqued. Encouraged by the comments of its members, I continued the story since I was pushed to do so by my husband Dean, the Rev. Richard Olson, Susan Swanson and Pam Boller.

I appreciate the technical support of my fourteen-year-old granddaughter Sarai and nine-year-old Elie who stood by patiently offering her help whenever required.

I'm grateful to Marey Todd and Dr. Gary Lucht for their enthusiastic endorsement and to the latter for his helpful suggestions.

However, if my friend and co-worker in Paraguay, Dr. Ruthie Sammons, had not undertaken the task of editing, lay-out and everything else connected with publishing, the manuscript would be destined to molder with other memorabilia, never to see the light of day.

Whoever dwells in the shelter of the Most High

will rest in the shadow of the Almighty.

I will say of the LORD,

"He is my refuge and my fortress,

my God, in whom I trust."

Psalm 91:1, 2

Margaret Lattin

ONE

The boy sat on the steps of the main building of the large factory complex watching the shadows creep slowly towards him. Everything became silent, only the steady steps of the guards on duty were audible.

"How long can I stay here without being missed?" he wondered. "Maybe forever," he thought. He stood up and looked around him. The same familiar sight met his eyes; only now, in the twilight, it appeared ominous. The tall, gray buildings sent a shiver down his spine, and the barbed wire fences surrounding the camp on three sides reminded him that he was their prisoner. On the fourth side, the river took away all hope for escape.

He walked over to a far corner of the grounds where he could see the grass and trees that were beyond his reach. He often sat there during the day imagining what lay beyond those woods, longing to slip under the fence to discover for himself that part of the world from which he felt excluded.

He thought about this so often that when the guard turned his back toward him, he daringly crawled under the bottom strand of wire fence. Having negotiated this feat successfully, he ran as fast as he could through the pine trees until he reached the far edge of the wood. There it was almost exactly as he had pictured it: a lovely green meadow stretched out before him. In the distance, the snow-capped mountains rose haughtily in their pristine splendor.

Exhausted from the uphill run, he flung himself on the ground. The smell of grass and soil restored his senses as he dug his fingers into the soft earth grasping for something within himself. Suddenly, he was torn back into reality by the sound of footsteps. Fear gripped him as he realized the consequence of his situation. "Have they followed me? Why didn't the guard stop me before this?" he thought.

Hesitantly, he rose to his feet to confront whatever fate lay before him. Instead of a guard's stern eyes like he had conjured up in his imagination, he looked into the friendly eyes of a young man in civilian dress. A sigh of relief escaped his trembling lips.

"My name is Franz," the stranger said. "I saw you running through those trees." A slight movement of his head indicated the direction. "Are you one of the refugee children who stay in the factory?" The boy was fascinated by the stranger's pronunciation of *Hoch Deutsch*. "Who are you?" Franz inquired. "There is a bench over there, let's sit down," he suggested. I live in the village of Adliswil. You see? There in the valley. I work as an auto mechanic in Zürich. May I presume that the answer to my question is yes?" The boy nodded his head.

"I stop by the camp often after work and watch the children play, but none have approached the fence close enough so I could talk to them. What is your name?"

"Paul."

"Paul. I like your name. There are many Swiss boys who have the same name as you. Have you met any Swiss boys yet?"

"No, I haven't."

"You will. This is only a temporary place for you to live. How many are there in your family?"

"Three."

"Three. What a coincidence; there are three in my family as well: my parents and I." Franz picked up a leaf from the ground, examining it in his hand.

"In our family, it's my mother, my sister and I."

"I see. Did something happen to your father in the war?" The boy stared at the ground.

"No, he died when I was one, when we still lived in Warsaw."

"You're from Poland then. How is it that you speak German?"

"Our mother is German, born in Poland. So were my grandparents."

The church bells ringing in the distance startled the two, and they jumped to their feet. The shadows had deepened. Reaching into his coat pocket Franz pulled out a bar of chocolate and handed it to Paul.

"I'll be waiting here for you every evening. Come whenever you can and bring your sister if your mother allows it. Later we'll have to think of a safer way to meet."

He watched the boy disappear into the trees, and then, slowly and in deep thought he made his way down the path to his car.

TWO

Totally oblivious to her surroundings she counted the stitches on her knitting needle. A look of annoyance flashed across the pallid face as a needle clattered onto the cement step, gathered speed, and rolled to the bottom. With cat-like agility she gathered the wool from her lap and raced to pursue it. Startled, she realized that it had gotten dark. A shiver jolted her slender frame. "Oh, Lord," she thought, "Where is Paul?" She remembered seeing him saunter towards the fence as he had done so often before, but never had he stayed out alone in the dark. Fear gripped her as her imagination suggested all sorts of things that could have happened to him. Ascending the steps two at a time, she reached the dingy room that had been home ever since that fateful night when they had crossed the border. The scene never varied from one day to the next. The burlap-covered straw mattresses lying on the floor stretched in unending rows before her. Army blankets were neatly folded on some, carelessly thrown on others. In one of the corners of the room several children were amusing themselves with self-made toys, while in another the older ones crowded around a story teller. Women gathered in small groups throughout the three-hundred-bed dormitory conversing in hushed voices. In one of the groups of youngsters she spotted the blond head of Jan. Swiftly she made her way toward him only to be disappointed by a shrug from him in response to her question: "Have you seen Paul?" The surroundings became blurry as she retraced her steps. Reaching the landing she spotted a small figure ascending the stairs. She sighed with relief. "Where have you been?" she spat out.

A sheepish grin and an outstretched hand holding something beautifully wrapped met her.

"What is it? Where have you been? Where did you get it? Do you have any idea how worried I have been?"

"I met a man whose name is Franz. He is Swiss, and he gave me this chocolate," he said dreamily as he pulled her to a seated position. He slowly recounted every detail of his adventure, taking no heed of the interruptions from his sister. "He'll be waiting for us in the same place tomorrow," he finally concluded. If he had hoped to avert her anger, he had miscalculated, for her pent up feelings of fear and neglected responsibility for him had to be vented. If, on the other hand, she had hoped to frighten him from meeting Franz, she too would be disappointed, for the nine year old squared his shoulders, looked at her defiantly and announced that if she would not go with him, he'd go without her. And with that he started to rip off the chocolate wrapper. She snatched the bar from him and carefully portioned out a few pieces to him, taking the same for herself. The children were convinced that they had never tasted anything so good in all their lives. Having missed supper, they devoured the chocolate and were still hungry. That hollow feeling in the pit of their stomachs never seemed to go away.

THREE

April 28, 1945, dawned drizzly and cold. The naked light bulbs in the women's and children's dorm had been switched on, casting their ghostly light upon the sleepers who began to stir, stretch and prepare to face another day. With a bound Paul threw off his blanket and made a dash for the latrine. A line had already formed. He stamped from one foot to the other— not only because of the urgency of the matter, but also to retain his body heat a little longer. Disinterestedly, he looked around expecting to see one of his friends. Instead, he noticed several men in striped uniforms who were always accompanied by guards. He had described these to his mother, calling them stern-faced scarecrows, and he still remembered the reprimand he had received from her. "They have suffered more than anyone in this camp," she had told him.

"Did it hurt to have those numbers tattooed on their arms?" he had asked. "Why are the guards always watching them? Do they want to hurt us?"

"The guards are watching them so that they don't harm themselves," she responded. "They have had such terrible things done to them and their families that the only way they know how to forget about them is to end their own lives."

His turn to go into the stall came—high time he thought.

Time had never passed so slowly before. No matter how he tried to amuse himself, Paul could only think of the encounter that lay before him that evening. It was difficult to concentrate on anything;

not only because of the prospect of meeting his friend again, but because his conscience was bothering him. Margaret, his sister who was two years his senior, was not in favor of his tryst with Franz. She had pointed out the dangers of such an undertaking and added that their mother would hardly approve of his wild scheme. Their mother had made it clear that in her absence he was to obey his sister. But despite Margaret's warning, when it started to get dark he was drawn as if by a magnet towards the northeast corner of the compound.

The rain had stopped in the early afternoon; only the shimmering of little pools collected in dips and hollows attested to its earlier occurrence. Every nerve strained as Paul watched the activity of the guards, waiting for that opportune moment when the guard would turn his back so that he could slither under the barrier. The leaves and pine needles were slippery, hindering him in ascending the hill. When he finally reached the crest, he thought for a moment that he was alone. Then, he caught a movement in the corner of his eye; and turning, he saw to his relief Franz rising from the bench and coming toward him.

"Tough going," Franz pointed out with a twinkle in his eyes as he surveyed the mud-covered shirt and shorts of the boy standing before him. "I see that your mother thought it best to wait for a dry day before allowing your sister to come."

"My mother doesn't know about this; she is in the hospital in Zürich."

"How long has she been there?"

"Three days already."

"Who looks after you?"

"Nobody, I can look after myself and Margaret." He straightened his shoulders and looked defiantly into his questioner's eyes.

"Margaret?"

"My sister, she is eleven."

"It's good that your sister has you to look after her. Let's sit down. I brought you something to eat. Are you as hungry as I am?" Franz unzipped his canvas bag and pulled out two sandwiches. He watched as Paul's disappeared—handing him his unfinished half.

****

As Franz noted how quickly the slim boy devoured the food he had brought, he realized that he had to do something to alleviate as much pain as he could from the boy's young life. This was brought home to him in the days to come when Paul more readily shared his story as his confidence in Franz grew. The deeper the Swiss' understanding of the refugee children's situation grew, the more he determined to get involved with this family. Franz had never dreamed that his casual observation of his country's involuntary involvement with the displaced persons (D P's) would lead to personal participation. At first, he had followed his town's conversion of the silk factory into a refugee camp from afar. As he had progressively noted the building of barricades, barbed wire fences, and later, the arrival of guards, and finally train loads of refugees, his interest in the proceedings grew. He observed as the war stealthily crept to his country's borders, waiting for that decisive moment to pounce upon its unsuspecting citizens. Was the establishment of a refugee camp in his neighborhood a step closer to becoming prey of the war machine? In time, his preoccupation with what might happen to him shifted to what had already taken place in the lives of the ones who landed on his doorstep. Each evening on his way home from work he had stopped and observed from afar the activities behind the barriers. He had even gone so far as to question the guards about what was going on. Their answers were inconclusive and puzzling. Either the powers that be didn't want their citizens to know what was going on, or else the guards themselves didn't know. What fascinated Franz most were the children gathered in little knots throughout the concrete covered area trying to amuse themselves in uncharacteristic quietness. He longed to communicate with them, to tell them that not all Swiss wore uniforms, carried rifles and talked gruffly. But the layout of the complex was not conducive to visitation. Thwarted in what he thought his mission to be, he stopped as usual on top of the hill to take in the glowing pink of the sunset's reflection on the snow covered Alps, and it was then that he first came face to face with the boy named Paul. He saw him emerge from the trees out of breath and sink into the grass. From the looks of him, and the direction from which he had emerged, Franz knew that he had come from the camp. This completely unforeseen event stunned him for a moment. He wondered if there was indeed a God who interested Himself in the lives of his creatures. Slowly, so as not to startle the prone figure, he advanced towards him and made an overture of friendship. When the boy answered him in his own language he was shocked. Perhaps many of the hundreds of children in that factory spoke German. It initially crossed his mind that this child might possibly be a child of the enemy. He did not know why he felt relieved when he discovered that the lad was from Poland.

It was at his second meeting with Paul that Franz determined he had to do something concrete to make future reunions above board. He told the boy that the next day, Saturday, he would try to locate him in the complex and he should tell his sister of his coming.

From that day until the disbandment of the camp, Franz would see that a little joy entered daily into the drab lives of the two children.

FOUR

It wasn't easy to persuade the officials of the camp to give Franz a pass to visit the children whenever it suited him. He also convinced the administration to allow him to take them off campus for short periods each day. He pointed out to the officer in charge that since the mother was in the hospital the children had no one to look after them. Equipped with the precious pass and the address of the hospital to which the mother had been admitted, he passed through the sentry-guarded gates into the dismal enclosure. He wondered how he would find Paul in those gloomy buildings facing him. That worry was soon eliminated, however, when he saw a small form separate itself from a group in a corner of the courtyard and speed towards him.

"So you have been watching for me," he grinned. The shining eyes that met his were better than any reward he could have imagined. And when the small hand was placed into his, tugging him gently into motion, warmth he had never known before permeated his whole being. Paul led him to the girl he assumed was his sister. She was of slight build, like her brother. Long braids framed her oval face in which the predominant features were the large fawn-colored eyes that examined him suspiciously. The shapeless dress, which hung loosely from her angular frame, made her appear older than eleven years old. The awkward silence was broken by Paul's enthusiastic introduction. "Margaret, this is my friend, Franz Vogel." On Paul's insistence they went to the place where he and his friend had first met. They sat on the familiar bench as Franz invited the children to a picnic.

Overwhelmed by the beauty which met her eyes, Margaret could hardly hold back her tears. She had forgotten that there was a world beyond the monotony and drabness of the camp that was home at the present. A carpet of green grass studded with delicate flowers in riotous colors lay at her feet.

She saw roofs of houses and church steeples, surrounded by trees, in the distance. Cows with golden bells at their throats were peacefully grazing, accompanied by the music of their bells. And on the horizon the majestic Alps reigned supreme over the kingdom at their feet. Franz watched in wonder as he saw the food he brought being devoured. He tried, with little success, to win Margaret's confidence. Only when he disclosed his plan for the afternoon, of going to the hospital to visit their mother, could he detect a little softening towards him.

Paul, sitting next to Franz in the bucket seat of the car, chatted on excitedly about the things he was seeing from the windows. From the back there was no sound. Negotiating the traffic in Zürich had not been Franz's first choice for a Saturday afternoon. However, because of his familiarity with the city they arrived at the hospital in good time.

FIVE

Up to this point of Franz' meeting the children he would never have dreamed of keeping a journal. The extent of his writing was to keep records in the shop where he worked. However, what he was experiencing now drove him to document what was happening, not only to the children, but more importantly, to himself. His parents only showed a superficial interest in the stories he brought home. After all, why should he be so excited about refugees when there were thousands like them to whom he could not reach out? Franz, however, felt that Providence had placed these two into his path; why, or for what purpose, he didn't know. Maybe if he put it into writing, a clearer picture would emerge.

"Today, I met Margaret. She is so intent and high strung that I wonder she hasn't snapped. I can only dimly imagine what has made her so fragile, and yet so wiry. Having the responsibility of her younger brother hasn't made life simpler for her. The mother being in the hospital is an added burden. From what Paul tells me, Margaret was very upset with his sneaking out in the evenings to meet me. I can only sympathize with her fears."

"Paul, on the other hand, has a wonderful resilience. His sanguine personality rebounds at the slightest provocation. He lives in the present, colorless though it is, gleaning from it what little pleasure it holds."

"I took the children to see their mother; it was the first time they had seen each other for over a week. As I watched the reunion of the three from the doorway, I felt that I needed to remove myself from this very moving scene. When I finally entered the room I was met with smiles and an introduction to the mother. I survived the embarrassment of the mother's sincere gratitude for my interest in her children. She said that I was God's answer to her prayers. Then I was subjected to Paul's detailed account of how we met, which resulted in the mother's expression of gratitude. I was encouraged to notice that Margaret's suspicion of me was gradually diminishing as she detected her mother's approval of me. There was lightness in her step when we left the hospital that hadn't been there before. The hint of a smile when I said good-bye at the camp's gate was my reward. "

****

During the next two weeks several visits to the hospital took place. In the first minutes of the reunion of mother and children, Franz usually sat silently, pretending to be absorbed in the scene outside the window. The children chatted excitedly; at least Paul did, about the things that had transpired since they last saw each other. They reported on picnics, walks, and swimming in the creek with their benefactor. After a while, the children often roamed the halls, reception rooms, and hospital grounds. This presented a chance for Franz to ask their mother some questions, showing his interest in the family's history. Slowly, a picture evolved of what had taken place up to the present time.

"Did you cross the border from Germany into Switzerland when it was opened to the refugees before the Allied invasion?" he asked. To which she responded:

"No, the border was not opened until the day after we crossed. Had we known about this, we could have spared ourselves a lot of grief. We lived in the small border town of Stühlingen. When we heard a rumor that the Allied forces were invading our town, we, along with most of the town's inhabitants, grabbed a few necessities and headed towards the near-by hill that constituted the border between Germany and Switzerland. It was cold and had been raining for the past few days. We were on the German side, heavily patrolled by their soldiers, and the Swiss had their guards along the other side. Between these two was no-man's land. The drizzly cold weather continued throughout the day. The Swiss were moved by the plight of the refugees. Towards late afternoon a group of civilians accompanied by men in uniform came to set up a tent. They also brought food and hot drinks. Everyone crowded into the shelter, grateful to get out of the inclement weather. However, it looked as if there was not enough room for all of us to be comfortable that night. We had lived in Stühlingen less than a year. A good part of that time we stayed on a farm. Because of this, we were only acquainted with a few of the town's dwellers. As it became apparent that the accommodations for the night would be insufficient, I felt a spirit of discontentment among several people. I noted from the start that they were not friendly towards us when I overheard someone asking who we were. We certainly were not welcome among these natives of the

Reich. This was curious as every man in our immediate family had lost his life to the Poles because they considered us to be German. Now, however, our German ancestry was not considered pure enough since we were born in Poland. When I became aware of the rumor that I might be a spy, I took my children and left the tent one dark night. My only thought was to get as far away as possible from the bigots who had allowed their compassion and fair play to die along with their idealism for the Fatherland."

"The rain had abated somewhat; but the low cloud-cover shut out any light from the moon or stars. The flashlight I had thrown into our luggage as an afterthought was of no use to us because it was imperative not to draw attention to ourselves. The signs along the border that promised death to anyone crossing were more than empty threats. Stumbling, slipping, and falling at times, we made our way deeper into the woods seeking shelter under a tall pine tree. I could never have taken the risk of endangering our lives, had I not relied on the guidance and protection of our Lord. I shudder when I think back to those miserable three nights and days we spent on that hill, without food, exposed to the elements. The hardest thing was the suffering of the children. Margaret seemed to have grasped the situation better and responded with her usual stoicism; but Paul, younger and more vulnerable, had a hard time adapting to the harsh reality of an empty stomach and a shelter-less, friendless existence.

"On the third day, I could no longer endure the suffering of the children, so I acted out a plan that had formed in my mind during the last few days. I observed that every day around noon a uniformed man rode along the Swiss border. I perceived that he was an officer checking on the patrolling guards. Braving the danger, I walked towards him, signaling to him as I went. To my relief, he responded, galloping towards me. I explained our predicament to him and was rewarded by his sympathetic ear. I told him of my desire to cross the border into Switzerland. I believe that God sent that particular man to help us escape a situation that was becoming unbearable. He told me that the Germans changed guards at midnight; and that for a few minutes during that time the border was not watched at a certain place. He carefully explained where this unguarded spot was, emphasizing once more the time for the undertaking. 'May God be with you' I heard him say as he rode away.

"Margaret held Paul's hand as I lifted a suitcase in each of mine. Cautiously, we made our way to where we were to cross. The night was crisp and clear. The moon lit the way ahead... at the same time making us visible to anyone sworn to guard the border. Reaching the designated crossing, we started to run in the direction I hoped was Switzerland. Suddenly we heard a stampede behind us. With my heart in my throat, I stopped to look around. Shortening the gap between us, I distinguished a group of men running in the same direction we were taking. As they pulled up beside us, out of breath, dirty, bleeding, their uniforms torn, the leader asked in Russian, 'Are we on Swiss soil?' During the First World War, my family had been refugees in Russia, so I had no problem understanding him. I answered that I wasn't sure where we were at the moment. The leader ordered the men to carry my suitcases, and grabbing the children's hands, we all continued running.

"Later, I learned that these men were prisoners of war who were being transported by train to a prison in Germany. In a place where the train passed along the Swiss border protected by barbed wire fences, they had jumped out.

"It seemed as though we had been running for a long time, although it couldn't have been very far, when to our utter horror we were ordered to halt. I knew that we couldn't expect mercy from a German guard. By God's grace, he was Swiss. He thoroughly interrogated us and then ordered me and the children to go back to where we had come from. After a lot of haggling back and forth, he eventually consented to my demand to see his superior. He grudgingly marched us to his commanding post, where we obviously were not expected. Nevertheless, after the briefest of questioning, in which I acted as interpreter for the Russians, a soldier took the children and me to a large storehouse where several guards prepared sleeping quarters for us. Their hospitality was almost overwhelming after the fear and stress we had endured. They brought us hot tea, bread and cheese. It seemed like a banquet."

****

We heard the children coming down the hall. This ended the story their mother was telling. I would have liked to hear more; however, this was a good stopping place. Mrs. Troper looked exhausted. In my journal that evening I noted that I was fascinated by the heroic story I had heard that afternoon, told by a remarkable woman. Her tenacity and courage surprised me. How could she undertake such daring actions? Ah yes, there was *Another* in her story, I almost forgot— One whom I admit I'd like to have on my side if ever I was called upon to risk three lives. I think I left the hospital with at least a partial answer to what attracted me to these children, and through them to their mother: that elusive quality of strength of character, that dignity which refused to be extinguished in circumstances that had worked to destroy them.

SIX

Mrs. Troper returned to Adliswil after more than a week at the hospital. She was occupied all day working as an interpreter for the administration of the camp. Franz continued to stop after work to do something special for the children, sometimes a walk outside the walls, or a chat on their bench on top of the hill. The rains became more infrequent and added periods of sunshine that awakened the wild flowers in the meadows. Rumors of suicides within the confines of the camp of people who had lost loved ones and their possessions and therefore had nothing to live for were lessening. Investigations of every person in camp continued to reveal that several S.S. officers and their families were among the refugees. These were immediately sent back to Germany.

When the news of the end of war reached the camp, it was met with tremendous joy. The city fathers in Adliswil were making overtures to dismantle the camp. Many refugees returned to their own countries, hoping to be reunited with their families and commence to rebuild their lives out of the ruins and destruction that they would encounter on their return.

Franz received the news about the war's end with mixed feelings. Questions arose in his mind that had no satisfactory answers. Where would his three protégées go? Their homeland was under communist rule. Whatever the long term solution, the present seemed uncertain for them. Presently, they would have to leave Adliswil. Relentless inquiry revealed that Paul and Margaret were being sent to a children's home in Trogen, a considerable distance from Zürich. A job as seamstress in a retirement home had opened for Mrs. Troper. Franz realized that an exception had been made for them because the rest of the D.P.'s were placed with farmers to work the land. If this arrangement was difficult for him to accept, then it was even harder for the three who had never been separated.

SEVEN

Franz took a day off from work the morning the trains with refugees were to leave for their various destinations. He located his friends on the crowded platform. For a moment he hesitated, hating to intrude. He wished that he hadn't come. He was tempted to break his promise that he made the night before when he had taken them into the city to an expensive restaurant. Located on a hill, it overlooked the Züricher See. Even though the air was chilly, the children wanted to sit on the terrace in order to watch the sailboats. All made a gallant effort to keep from alluding to the topic of imminent separation. At the end, they had not said good bye. "We'll see each other at the train station," he had told them; and he was rewarded by their grateful smiles. He willed himself to move towards them. Paul, who had been watching out for him, detached himself from his mother and sister and started sprinting towards him. He dodged back and forth between luggage and people until he reached him. Franz felt a small hand placed into his. He allowed himself to be gently pulled into the direction of the others. Brave smiles belied the fact of the parting that lay ahead. He produced colorful parcels he had brought for the children, giving instructions not to open them until the train left the station. The rest of the time, until the children boarded the train with a young social worker who was to accompany them, was now a blur. He went with Mrs. Troper to her platform and waited until that train left also. Then he made his way to the car.

In the kitchen he poured himself a stein of beer and took it to his room. Throwing off his jacket and tie, he gulped down the cold liquid. It tasted flat and bitter. Collapsing on his bed with hands behind his head, he starred at the ceiling. A loneliness he had never felt before overcame him. As he drifted into a state of non-reality where he felt himself floating between two worlds, he replayed in his head the conversations he had with Mrs. Troper:

****

"How did you get to Germany from Poland?" he had asked the diminutive woman sitting next to him on the barrack's steps. Her gray eyes looked deep into his as if to discern if he really wanted to know or if he merely wished to satisfy his curiosity.

"That is a long story; I hardly know where to begin. My husband Jacob was a missionary working in Warsaw with the Jewish people, supported by a mission organization in England. The salary we were receiving barely met our needs. We lived in a three room apartment and I never knew whom Jacob would bring home to share whatever was needed with that person. I had to learn to stretch our food so none of the guests went away hungry. It was an exciting life! I met such interesting people and experienced true fulfillment by sharing with others what little we had. Of course, I was often irritated with my husband when I looked into his closet and discovered missing articles of clothing that he had given away even though he hardly could do without them. The only thing I remember that he would have liked for himself was a typewriter. He was taking a correspondence course from Chicago, Illinois, and he felt it would be helpful if he typed the material he had to send back. I found a way to fulfill his wish by holding back a bit of grocery money each month with which I bought a second-hand machine for his birthday. I can still see how happy and surprised he was, and it sustains me when sorrow threatens to crush me. It was soon after this when I stood helplessly at his hospital bed watching him slip away from us. He had gone to the barber to get a haircut. The barber cut through an infection he had on his neck. I noticed shortly after that he walked with his head to one side. When he complained of a stiff neck, I insisted he should see a doctor. He was checked into the hospital where several physicians consulted about his case. The majority decided to operate. Three days later he was dead. The diagnosis was blood poisoning. He was twenty-six years old. We had been married four years. It was September 1937. How could God let a righteous man die who had done so much good for Him? I stormed, I raved, and I groveled! I felt that God had forsaken us. The mission board suggested since I was a young widow I ought to work to support myself. The children, they thought, would be best cared for in an orphanage. Can you imagine placing my two into an orphanage—they weren't orphans, they still had a mother! I don't know how I managed to function during the days that followed. I was a boat without an anchor, headed towards a rocky shore. In the background, however, a still small voice reminded me: "be still and know that I am God." I have experienced since then that God does not always choose to give answers to our demands, but by His grace He answered mine. A little later when I was ready to listen, the answer came. It was more terrible than I imagined—it came September 1, 1939. He was better off than we were going to be."

****

A bolt of lightning…followed by rumbling thunder…brought Franz back to the present. He jumped off his bed to close the window against the storm. No hope for sleep now. No matter how much he tried, he couldn't get Mrs. Troper's voice out of his head.

****

"My parents lived on a small farm fifty kilometers from the capital and so did the rest of my family. My oldest sister had immigrated to the United States when she was eighteen years old. I was four at the time. My parents and several friends lent me money to invest in a modest grocery store in Warsaw. Together with two employees we managed to build it up by degrees. Our apartment was directly in back of my business, facilitating the management of the household and the supervision of Margaret and Paul.

"My day started at four in the morning at which time I received the milk delivery. This was followed by the baker who brought his goods. It did not take long for my clients to spread the word to others that their grocer measured their weights honestly. Also, the bread and dairy products were fresh. The business grew until I was able to invest in a retail store as well. Of course there were many prejudices to overcome. I was a woman and I was not a true Pole, even though I and my parents and grandparents were born in Poland. The latter objections increased as the war rumors intensified. Money no longer a factor, we moved to a three bedroom apartment in an affluent part of the city. It had a balcony leading out of the living room that afforded an expansive view of the neighborhood. We had come a long way from the dilapidated part of town where we had lived before. I could buy the latest toys for my children as well as expensive clothes. However, I would have exchanged all this without hesitation for my former life with Jacob. How I missed him! The business demanded my full attention and energy so that there wasn't much opportunity for reminiscing. Nevertheless, the nights and Sundays brought back the raw pain. Most Sunday afternoons the children and I went to the cemetery. In fact it was there where Paul took his first steps.

"I don't need to tell you about Hitler's invasion of Poland; I'm sure you have followed that closely in your newspapers, but what I can tell you is how we were affected by it. To my surprise, a neighbor of my parents showed up at my store one morning with the news that my family wanted me to come home. Something terrible had occurred. He refused to reveal any details. I left the business and the children in our employee's care and boarded the first train home. My family lived close to the Vistula River, so I could go part way by ship and the last few kilometers by foot. I imagined all sorts of calamities that had taken place to necessitate the urgent summons. However, nothing prepared me for what awaited me. I couldn't see any physical changes as I walked along the familiar path in the twilight. The fields were lying peacefully on both sides of the unpaved road. Trees in the orchards were heavily laden with fruit. The houses, most of which were inhabited by people I knew, were unaltered. I was tempted to stop at my brother's farm which was only a little out of my way, but an urgency to discover the news drove me on.

"Nostalgia overcame me as I spotted the stork's nest perched on the thatched roof of my childhood home. It had been a long time since I had thought about these giant birds that had chosen one of the gables of our house to build their nests. Oil lamps were being lit as I reached our picket gate. The path leading to the house was defined by round, whitewashed stones and tall poles entwined in green beans climbing up on them.

"My father met me at the door before I had taken the last step; he pulled me into the foyer. I had never seen him so solemn. He took me into his arms and stroked my hair. Without a word he led me into the kitchen where my mother, sister and sister-in-law were sitting around the table, crying. Ida jumped up from the window seat and rushing toward us shrieked: 'they have killed Eduard and Reinhard.' In a stupor, I sank to the nearest chair.

The funeral for my brother and brother-in-law took place the following afternoon. The latter's casket remained closed because the body had been mutilated beyond recognition. My only brother, on the other hand, lay peacefully as if asleep, a shadow of a smile playing on his lips. Few homes had their young men spared from this atrocity.

Those homes that did, didn't know in which prison their loved ones were rotting.

"I learned that this massacre had been committed by the Poles, who showed up armed in the tranquil village and demanded that all fighting age men must come with them to Warsaw. The round-up was swift and complete. The procedure was duplicated in all villages where people of German descent were living since the time of Katherine the Great who had invited German farmers to settle the land. The men were not allowed to take anything with them. Mercilessly they were driven on foot 50 kilometers without food or water to the prison in Warsaw. Only the strongest survived the march. Anyone not keeping up the pace was beaten and shot. My nephew and niece, the same age as my two children, lost both their father and their uncle on the same day. For the first time, I was glad that my sister Paula had no children. My mother had cried until there were no tears left. Now she showed a stoic face through all of this. How much more grief will this tiny, wiry woman have to face in these days of imminent war, I wondered?"

EIGHT

Franz shuddered involuntarily as he remembered the pain in the voice of his story teller.

"By the time I got back to Warsaw, I could hear shooting in the distance. I was told that the city was surrounded by the enemy. Shortly after the dairy and bakery delivery, all stores were ordered to close. The inhabitants were warned to stay off the streets. I ordered my helpers to carry as much food as they could from the shop to our apartment, while I filled the bathtub with water. This proved to be providential because the water and gas lines were later shut off—the city had capitulated to the Germans.

"We began noticing strange things happening around us. People were so hungry that they rushed out of their houses with knives in hand when a horse fell on the street. They started cutting even before the animal had died. Customers continually came to our door asking for something to eat. Too soon our supplies were dwindling away. When one of my helpers joined the horse butchering crowd I did not prevent her. However, I did not join the family at the table for the horse-meat dinner.

"The Polish resistance fought bravely to save our city, but they were no match for the German forces. Our life-style changed again. First we were asked to give up one of our rooms to a German engineer. Fortunately, it was only a room. Many had their houses and whole apartments confiscated. Because we were of German ancestry we had privileges that the Poles didn't. However, we were not looked upon as true Germans born in the Fatherland. Instead, we were called *Volksdeutche*—a step down from the elite. Then Margaret and Paul were required to attend a school taught by German teachers. They never learned to read or write in Polish. Only with friends and neighbors did they speak that language.

"Herr Ritterhof, our boarder, was a good-hearted man who missed his family very much. He generously supplemented our groceries which, of course, were rationed. Margaret and Paul reminded him of his own children, so he enjoyed their company whenever he had some free time.

"We attended a church which was located in a section of town predominantly inhabited by Jewish people. I noticed one Sunday what looked to be a building project. The following week a section of a wall started to materialize. This progressed at great strides from week to week. Curious to learn what purpose this structure served, I asked one of the soldiers supervising the workers. He gruffly rebuffed me, telling me that I should go about my business and not concern myself with things I knew nothing about. Later when I questioned our house guest, he pleaded ignorance. He did, however, warn me to stay away from that part of the city.

"After my husband's death I had only infrequent contact with friends from the mission. I spent most of my time and energy making a living for the three of us. Of course, I was appalled by the speeches I heard on the radio and the conversations of the Poles in which I detected increasing anti-Semitism.

"However I couldn't believe that hatred could go to such extents as to wall-in a people. One evening one of our former co-workers stopped to visit. Rachmiel had taken over my husband's work after he died. The stories he related of what was taking place to his compatriots since the German take-over shocked me to the core. He counseled me to be careful about letting anyone know of our association with Jews. The knowledge of the suffering of my friends added to the heavy burden of my daily tasks. There were numerous times I acted as a liaison between the Germans and the Poles who were my customers or friends when they were in trouble due to some infringement that the occupiers imposed or because of a misunderstanding. Often I was able to help them, not only because I was Volksdeuche, but also because our house guest had put a good word in for me with the authorities. However, when I consulted with him about helping my Jewish friends, he made it quite clear that he would not be able to do anything on their behalf.

"Not infrequently, on my way to work I encountered horrible sights which made me aware of the nightmare in which we lived. A daring Pole would take a shot at a man in uniform, and the Germans in turn retaliated by lining up passersby against a wall and shooting them. Usually the guilty person had fled, and those taking his punishment had nothing to do with the crime. I can still hear the shots ringing in my ears.

"From time to time a skeletal child showed up at our door begging for bread. These were Jewish children who somehow had slipped past the guards of the Ghetto. On the way home from one of my stores a red-headed man came up behind me and addressed me by name. It took me a while to recognize Rachmiel. He had dyed his hair and carried forged papers. He asked to stay the night. The previous nights he had been hiding in a wood shop, sleeping in a casket. It was no longer safe for him there. I invited him to come with me, and the following morning I made arrangements for several other hiding places. He intended to flee Poland as soon as possible.

NINE

A shutter banged against the window casing. The darkness of Franz' room was illuminated for a split second. The crash of thunder reverberated through the house. Throwing off his clothes he slipped between the cool sheets. Finally he slept.

After work he visited the old haunts he and the children had frequented, replaying in his mind the conversations, reliving impressions, recreating the ever changing expressions on their faces. It astonished him how little it took to make them happy and how much satisfaction he received from seeing them act like children again. He tried tenaciously to hold on to the picture of them playing ball together, splashing each other in the river, scampering along the hiking path or savoring the chocolates. Nevertheless, behind those happy scenes there lurked the one at the railroad station—separation, loneliness, and fear.

And then, that long awaited letter written in the unsteady hand of the child arrived:

"Dear Uncle Franz, it's nice here in Trogen. Above the front door a painted sign says: *Kinderheim Morgenlicht.* You can see from my drawing, which is not very good, how the Children's Home looks." He searched the envelope for the drawing, but there was none.

"There is a little stream in a deep gorge that flows by the Heim. I like listening to it because it reminds me of the walks we took, you and Paul and I by the creek in Adliswil. In front of the house a road goes by where cars and motorbikes and hay wagons pass. In back there is a lovely meadow and fruit trees. The tree I like best is to the right of the house, it is very big. It's an oak tree and it has a bench all around it. Once in a while it is my turn to sit on the bench beside Fraulein Doris Fülleman when she tells a story. The rest of the children sit on the grass and listen. We take walks together through the meadows and there also is a small forest nearby."

There followed a whole line that was blacked out. Then the letter went on: "When the bell rings in the morning we jump out of bed and wash up right in our bedroom in bowls filled with water. Then we rush downstairs for breakfast at long tables. I like the soft white bread and butter, but it takes me longer to eat the porridge. Dr. Wasserman, the lady who is in charge, says that Paul eats too fast and that he must count to one hundred before he swallows each mouthful so his stomach won't ache. I want to tell you now about the best thing that happened to me: When I came upstairs to our bedroom one evening I saw a lovely little doll on my bed. She looked just like "Rotköpfchen" waiting for the basket to be given to her to take to her grandmother who lived in the woods. I am so happy to have that doll all to myself. I want her to have a Swiss name, so I asked Tante Doris (that is Fraulein Fülleman) what I could call the doll. She told me several names, but in the end we decided on Vrenely. I also asked Tante Doris how the doll came to be sitting on my bed. She said one must learn to accept gifts without having to know who gave them. Paul says I must not forget to greet you from him. I greet you too." Another crossed out line and then the signature. So there was Fraulein

Fülleman. What would Mrs. Troper call her— an angel unawares? He could not remember the exact words, but he was happy for Margaret.

It was not easy for Franz to write letters. His life was too ordinary to be of interest to the children. He was becoming more aware of the everyday things around him, always looking for something that he could share with them. He took to heart his own advice that he had given them to go to a 'pretty place' each day. They had made a game of it when they had been together. At first he had to point out the things that are often taken for granted: the beauty of ordinary things. His students were fast learners and delighted him with objects that appeared special to them. The letter he just read showed that Margaret was sensitive to her surroundings. If he doubted that, his concern was completely dispelled by the next letter in which she described an excursion to the mountains.

"…..the bell rang when it was still dark. We were going to make the day last a long time. Tante Doris said to us yesterday that we were going to the Alps. Paul and I have never been on the Alps. All of us went, except Lydia who was staying to do something special with Dr. Wasserman. Lydia has braces on her legs and can't climb the Alps. First we took a truck for about five minutes to the village of Trogen. There we boarded the train and later a cog-rail that went up slowly on the mountain slope. I was afraid that we might slip backwards and go crushing down the mountain. But Tante Doris said that these trains never had an accident. When I heard this I wasn't so afraid and I started looking for a "pretty place." I found it everywhere. We were winding around through trees, but when we came to places where there weren't any trees, we could see the Alps in the distance, but much closer than in Adliswil. Pretty soon they started glowing pink from the rising sun. I thought we were in heaven. When we came to the end of the cog-rail line, we walked up even higher. All along the way there were flowers: Alpine roses, dark blue gentians, yellow and white flowers. There was a restaurant up there at the station too, but we didn't stop. When we came to the highest part we could see the tops of the Alps in Austria. Can you envision that we were above a layer of clouds? Well, Uncle Franz, what I saw that day is going to make up for a lot of "pretty places."

"Mutti wrote that there are lovely woods behind the big hospital where she works. She goes wandering in them during her lunch break, and she can see them out of her window when she sits at the sewing machine. I like to think of her wandering through the forest, don't you?

"Paul has found a best friend, Peterly, but I…." the next lines were blacked out, and then the signature.

Franz wondered what she had been trying to convey to him in the section that was expunged. He noticed that the letters were neatly written and correctly spelled. He suspected that they were copied from a rougher draft and corrected by someone; and therefore, they were most likely censored; probably by Dr. Wasserman. The absence of any reference to her pre-Swiss days was not surprising, since she had never referred to them in their previous conversations. Whatever he had learned about their history had been through Paul, although very sketchy, and of course from Mrs. Troper. She seemed to be relieved to be able to share her experiences with someone. He could still hear her saying:

"Of course, our relatively routine life came to an abrupt end when the Russians were approaching our borders. Bombing of Warsaw became the order of the day and even more at night. We no longer undressed when going to bed because we expected the sirens screaming up and down our streets warning us to seek shelter. The house we lived in had no basement, so we were forced to run across the street to the nearest one. Several people were hit by the explosion or shrapnel as they made their way to safety. The suspense of the whistling bombs tearing through the air was the worst. Where were they going to hit? If we got out alive after this attack, would there be a home to go to? The unimaginable that could happen would be to be separated from my children. I saw this happen over and over as parents were killed and their children left alive, or vice versa. During the most concentrated attacks I placed my head on that of Margaret, whose head was on Paul—none of us or all of us, I pleaded with the Lord. Everyone reacted differently to these potential dangers. Some were screaming; others crying or counting their rosary beads, while others remained in stoic silence. Margaret's reaction was the latter. Paul, on the other hand, whimpered and begged me to pray whenever he noticed that my eyes were open. "

Franz could picture the scene being described—the three cowering in a cold dark cellar, paralyzed by fear of what the next moment had in store for them.

TEN

"**Y**ou asked how we had managed to come to Germany from Poland, she had said. "I'm finally answering your question.

"There was a large hospital in Warsaw designated for wounded German soldiers. Their numbers increased at an alarming rate. German speaking women were required to volunteer several hours a week to help cheer up these men and keep up their morale. The volunteers wrote letters for those who had lost their hands, arms or eyes. They read to them, conversed with them, and in short, tried to help them to make the best of their situation. I was assigned to the ward of those who were not likely to survive. I had experience! I had watched my husband die. This did not make it any easier, however. First of all, my husband had no fear of death. He knew that he was going to his loving heavenly Father. Most of the boys at whose bedside I sat had no such hope; instead they were in the grips of fear of what was awaiting them beyond the fragile thread to which they were desperately clinging. My words of consolation carried little weight, but I had the Word of God which promised forgiveness of sin, a life in the presence of God after death, a reunion with loved ones, and the presence of the good Shepherd to accompany them through the valley of the shadow of death. The ones who chose to believe what God's Word stated were rewarded with peace.

"When I arrived at the bedside of one of my boys I found that he had visitors from Germany. It was his brother and sister-in-law. They were strangers to Warsaw and therefore happy to accept my help in finding accommodations and information about places to eat, shop etc. Before they returned to their homeland, after the death of their loved one, they invited me to come and stay with them if the situation in Warsaw should deteriorate. They lived in a small village on the Swiss border that had been mostly spared from enemy bombs.

"After one of the bombings in which 40,000 people were killed in one night in the capital alone, I obtained a pass to take my children to my parent's home. I left them there and returned to the city because I couldn't leave my business unattended for long periods of time. I was glad to think that Margaret and Paul were in a relatively safe place. They loved their holidays in the country with their grandparents, aunts and cousins. After returning from one of these visits I received word that my father had died of a heart attack. This had been completely unforeseen, since he never complained about any pain. His passing was a great loss, not only to his family, but also to the community. Margaret was especially hard hit because she had been Father's favorite.

"When we came back from the funeral, our house guest informed us that the Russian army was advancing towards Warsaw. He predicted an imminent evacuation of all German civilians and suggested that we should take advantage of this opportunity to leave the city.

"We made our last journey to my childhood home to bid farewell to it and what was left of my family. Saying good-bye to my mother and relatives was a heartrending experience. I tried to persuade them to join us, but they, the eternal optimists, couldn't imagine that it would get any worse than it had already been. They wanted to remain on their farms. I had never seen my mother show so much emotion as when she said good-bye to us. "We'll see each other again," I tried to reassure her. "When this war is over, we'll get together somehow." My mother's fatalistic outlook, however, did not change. She did not believe that there would be a reunion on this earth. Tearfully, she handed me a side of bacon. "Take it with you, Martha; you'll never know how useful it may be." Reluctantly I made room for it in my already bulging luggage, never dreaming of its enormous benefit in the days to come.

"Returning to our apartment in Warsaw we waited for the order of evacuation, which came a few days later. I was leaving behind my family, my business, a comfortable apartment, a life I had won from hard work and sleepless nights. I took a last look at my living room when I noticed something missing from it. It was the tablecloth that usually covered our round table. I had stuffed it into my suitcase as a souvenir. Taking it out of the suitcase, I placed it back to where it belonged. Only then did I close the door, knowing I would never see my home again.

"The train that pulled out of the Central Station in the dead of night was filled mainly with the families of military personnel destined for their homeland. There were no happy faces among the passengers. Most wives were leaving behind their husbands to an unknown fate. At the same time, they didn't know what to expect once they returned to their devastated homes. Luggage had been limited to what could be carried by each individual. There was barely any seating available. Children were either held on laps or perched on suitcases in the already narrow aisles. A palpable feeling of foreboding hung heavily in the compartment we were occupying.

"We had barely crossed the border into Germany when our train was confiscated to transport wounded soldiers. Now it was everyone on their own trying to arrange transportation. This, of course, was almost impossible since all vehicles were used to move the troops. We attempted to make ourselves comfortable on the hard benches at the train station. While the children were fitfully sleeping, I circulated among the railroad officials asking questions, telling them of our plight, begging, even bribing but all to no avail. I discovered that I had no bargaining power since all the money had become completely worthless. Our situation became desperate when Paul became very ill. His temperature seemed to mount by the hour. More trains arrived and their passengers were abandoned at the station which was much too small to hold everyone. The village had no accommodations; hotels no longer existed. Only rubble and gaping holes were in their place. The droning of B -17's sent everyone scurrying to find a place to hide. The sound of explosions was deafening. The ground shook beneath us. Screams from the vicinity of the train were heart wrenching. When we returned to the bullet riddled carriage it was readied for departure. Once again I approached the station master, this time offering him a piece of the bacon my mother had given. Miraculously he accepted it, promising us a place on the train. At the last minute before it pulled out he signaled us to board. We squeezed into the aisle, stepping over prone bodies that shifted slightly, making room for the suitcases which became our seats. The train had gone only a short distance before the sky became alive with the dreaded sound of airplanes. Every able bodied person scattered into the countryside. Returning after the attack there was more room in the aisles. Several of the wounded were killed by machine-gun fire from the air. By now Paul's hot body was lying motionless on my lap. I had the address of a pastor friend who lived in a city on our route. We found our way to our friend's tiny apartment. He arranged for us to stay at a hotel near-by. He directed me to a physician who had been too old to be drafted into the army's medical core. In a week my son was fit to travel again.

"All trains moved under cover of darkness. During daylight we hid whenever possible in forests. Even there we were not safe from the strafing enemy fires. It took three weeks of traveling before we reached our destination of the Hagely's farm in Stühlingen.

"Mr. Hagely had been drafted into the *Wehrmacht*, leaving his wife to run the farm. Even though I had been brought up on a farm, I never had to concern myself with anything on it except the flower garden or helping mother in her vegetable plot. However, now I was called upon to take care of the cow, which happened to be a very stubborn one. At times, when I was taking her out to pasture, she insisted on getting onto the railroad trestle, subjecting me to run huffing and puffing after her, switch in hand. More than once she narrowly escaped being hit by a train. It was too nerve wracking to drive the cow to the meadow, so I decided to bring the grass to her. Taking the scythe over my shoulder, I headed for the pasture.

However, I soon discovered that mowing grass was a whole lot more difficult than it appeared. I was on the point of giving up when I heard a voice behind me.

"Is this the first time you've used a scythe?" It was a border guard who had been watching me. He laid down his rifle, and in no time at all he mowed enough grass for me to take to the obstinate animal.

"The work that needed to be done each day seemed unending. Frequently, I accompanied my and the Hagely children to the potato fields where we gathered up the tubulars into sacks to be lugged back into the vegetable cellars. With few exceptions our backbreaking task was interrupted by the buzz of approaching airplanes. We threw ourselves onto the ground as the low flying bombers flew over us.

"One day Mr. Hagely showed up unexpectedly. He had deserted the army. Now that the head of the family was back to take charge of the farm, I started looking for a place to rent in the village nearby. A two room make-shift attic apartment would have to do for us. It was sparsely furnished. A wood burning belly stove in one of the rooms was the only source of heat available. This was also to serve as a cook stove. As winter was approaching I used some of the pieces of clothing I had brought along from my store in Warsaw to exchange for down and feathers from which I made comforters to keep us warm during the frigid nights in the unheated bedrooms.

"Soon the articles which I had for bartering were at an end. I needed a job! The only work available in Stühlingen was at a factory that manufactured soldiers' shirts. This meant being away from the children all day. I prayed for the Lord's wisdom to show me how to resolve this situation to a favorable outcome. I believe that He allowed the supervisor of the factory to empathize with our circumstances and to suggest that I sew the shirts at home. I did this while the children read, did their homework or played near the potbellied stove on cold winter days. In the evenings I accompanied the children to school and then picked them up when their classes were over. It was too dangerous to be on the streets in the daytime because most of the air attacks took place during the day.

"Christmas was especially difficult that year. There was nothing to buy in stores that could pass as Christmas presents. I tried to prepare Paul and Margaret that the Christ child would bring nothing that year because it was war. I'm not sure if they believed me since they had been taught that nothing is impossible for God to do. Besides sewing for the factory, I occasionally altered clothes for people whom I knew. I had restyled a coat for our landlady and kept the small remnant. After the children went to bed, I made a cape with a hood from the lovely plaid fabric for Margaret's doll. We had brought the doll from Poland because it was given to her by her father. I also had done some alterations for the town's carpenter, who instead of paying for it, agreed to make a small truck for Paul. I procured a small fir tree which I decorated with colorful spools of thread and glistening paper ribbons. The children stared open-mouthed when they entered our all-purpose room. I think they were happier with these simple gifts than they had been with the expensive ones they had received in times past. The Christmas story took on a new meaning for the three of us that bitter lonely December 24th. We understood to a small degree the meaning of what was said about Jesus: that though He was rich He became poor for us that through His poverty we might become rich.

"Then came the day when we heard that an army was to invade our village. We, along with the rest of the inhabitants, fled into the forest on top of the nearby hill. The rest you already know."

Franz remembered hanging on to every word Mrs. Troper was saying. Only when she had finished her reminiscing had he realized that he was stiff from sitting so long in the same position. He had thanked the story teller for sharing her experiences with him and had asked if he could come back for more. The request was graciously granted.

ELEVEN

From time to time, at unexpected moments, there flashed into Franz' mind a scene from one of Mrs. Troper's narratives, so vivid and tangible that it felt as if he were a participant. He tried to imagine the long range impact the past had made on her and her children. Compared with his own life he felt like a cocoon from which he now wanted to escape and come forth as a transformed human being. One that was cognizant of the privileged existence in which he moved and at the same time able to empathize with those who were denied their basic rights. He longed to vicariously experience what the D. P.'s had suffered in order to dispel the monotony and purposelessness of his own existence. He had written to the Kinderheim Morgenlicht requesting permission to visit, but the response had not been encouraging. However he was not going to be daunted by the noncommittal answer. Meanwhile, there was no restriction to seeing their mother.

The Sunday morning he chose to visit Ittigen, near Bern, dawned to a laden sky threatening rain. Franz had hoped for a view of Eiger, Mönch and Jungfrau, the three mountains dominating the Berner Oberland. They never failed to amaze him by their spectacular majesty. The wet pavement and limited visibility forced him to give his full attention to negotiating the uneven highway. Arriving in Ittigen shortly before noon, he could see the outlines of the imposing building of the Asyl Gottesgnad on the side of the hill which ascended steeply from the village. Mrs. Troper met him in the foyer with her perpetual smile that extended to her expressive gray eyes. After exchanging greetings, she led him to the dining room where lunch was served. He was introduced to several of the sisters in their somber black dresses and starched white caps. Seated between Mrs. Troper and one of the nurse's aides he overheard a conversation taking place across from him by one of the ladies speaking with a thick French accent. Sylvia, he learned later, was from the province of Turino, Italy, to which the Huguenots fled when persecuted for their protestant faith. Painfully aware of being the only man in the room, he was relieved when Mrs. Troper led him to the lounge where most of the afternoon the two were left undisturbed. Comfortably seated in an easy chair opposite Mrs. Troper, he felt at ease anticipating the conversation that was to follow.

"So, are you happy here, apart from missing your children?" he asked.

"Oh, yes, I like the work and the people are very kind. You didn't meet the head seamstress with whom I spend most of my time. She tries very hard to make me feel welcome here. Then there is Sylvia, who sees to it that we have something to smile about. And then there are the patients who are always so grateful for the time I spend with them."

"Do you work on the wards as well?" he asked surprised.

"Yes, every morning before breakfast I assist in serving meals to the ones who are bed-ridden. Then after I eat, I start sewing. In the evenings I help get the patients into bed."

"You don't have much time for yourself, do you?"

"Sundays are my days off, and during my lunch hour and in the evenings I take long walks in the little woods that are on three sides of the Sanatorium. I love that time, but that's also when I miss my children the most. I wish that they could be right here with me. But the head-sister has pointed out that the environment among old people would not be suitable for children. I have contacted the immigration department to see if they could place Paul and Margaret into a private home near Ittigen. They have agreed to look for such a place, but so far they have only found people who are willing to take one of them. I, however, will not allow them to be separated." She wiped a tear from her eyes.

"I agree with you that to separate the two would be harmful." He continued on with what he hoped was a safer subject: "Have you heard anything from your family in Poland?"

"Yes, I have letters from both of my sisters. From what I can read between the lines, things are in a state of chaos. They don't come right out and say so because they fear censorship of the mail, but it must be terribly difficult for all of them. My mother is living with my youngest sister, Olga, in Lotz. She has five children and has heard nothing from her husband since he was drafted into the army after surviving the march to the Warsaw prison. When the Germans took over he was given a uniform and sent to Russia to fight on that front. I suspect that he was killed, but Olga still hasn't given up hope of seeing him again. Mother lives with them because most of the farms of the Germans have been confiscated by the Poles. The farm of my brother was taken over by the hired hand that had the audacity to offer my sister-in-law a position as maid if she and her two children wanted to remain on their property. I have found all this out from one of their neighbors who had been allowed to leave Poland and go to Germany. Paula, my older sister, still lives in her home, but she has to give almost all of the things produced to the government. She hardly has enough left for herself. As I said before, my mother lives with Olga. She takes care of Olga's five children so that my sister can work for the Poles in order to buy food for the family. Living in a big city, away from her farm, must be difficult for my mother. Whenever she visited us in Warsaw, she would take walks past the flower shops and gaze at the displays of plants which reminded her of home.

"I have been sending packages of sugar, flour, beans and coffee to Olga. These will help a little, but inside these staples I have hidden silk stockings. If she can sell these on the black market she might have a chance of survival." Her eyes twinkled merrily, "You see, we haven't gone through these hard times for nothing; through them we have learned a few tricks on which often our lives depend." Her infectious laugh reinforced the admiration Franz held for this tenacious woman.

Suddenly her demeanor changed. The light from those expressive gray eyes faded into discernible pain. A sigh escaped her compressed lips before she went on with her story:

"I have had news that my seventeen-year-old cousin, who also had been drafted into the army, was killed in Stalingrad. He was a conscientious objector, as most of our men were. I dread to tell Margaret the news; she was a great admirer of him. He lived with his parents and a sister diagonally across the street from my parents. The children saw a lot of Max, who even though older, was fond of them. He took them on hikes and camping trips. When I reflect on the fact that every man in my immediate family died a violent death during this war, I thank God for sparing my husband from that fate."

A man in a wheel chair entered the lounge. He smiled as he exchanged greetings with Mrs. Troper and Franz, and he joined the two of them. The conversation changed to present happenings. Others came in and out of the room. At one of the tables a card game was organized. The man in the wheel chair joined the players. The two resumed their conversation.

"Tell me about your childhood home and your family. How did it happen that you understood the Russian prisoners of war with whom you came in contact at the border?"

"Aren't you getting tired of hearing me talk all the time? As you notice, I don't run out of things to say." She rearranged the pillow at her back.

"I like listening to you! You open up an entirely new world to me."

"A world I'm glad you did not have to live in, although it is interwoven with beauty and joy as well. I only have to close my eyes to see the home where I grew up and where so many happy moments took place." Her dreamy look substantiated her remark. Franz settled back into his chair in anticipation. He was not disappointed. How could he possibly imagine what it was like to grow up in a place so foreign from what he had been used to.

TWELVE

"I see a house of roughhewn lumber. It is built on a slight incline. A pathway leads from the unpaved street to the front of the house. On both sides of this path, outlined by white-washed river rocks, are high bean stocks. Several steps lead to the open porch on which a bench is located in front of the kitchen window. It is not unusual to smell the aroma of bread baking as one steps into the flag stone hall. Directly in front is the oven, which is built into the brick wall. My mother is standing in front of it with a long-handled wooden trowel extracting the fragrant, crusty round loaves to feed her family of six. The double doors at the right open to the meeting room where each Sunday the village inhabitants join our family for worship. The guest room, where traveling preachers often stay, is beyond the sanctuary. The door on the left leads into the heart of the home, the kitchen, which also serves as the family living room. The iron cooking stove provides heat during the subzero weather. On the other side of the room is a window alcove with a table and built-in bench. The latter, when the lid is lifted up, serves as a bed for me and my brother. On the side are shelves that hold my mother's dishes and cooking utensils. At the far end of the room is the solid wood bed and dresser of my parents. Running along the same wall as the kitchen is a narrow corridor leading to a door on the left. It is our barn. In it there are two cows and several pigs as well as chickens and ducks. Straight ahead is my father's domain—the cobbler shop. Not only are his sewing machines, work bench, and tools located here, but also a bed. Often he prefers to sleep among his familiar surroundings instead of the hubbub of the kitchen where he is woken in the middle of the night by a crying baby from the crib by the side of the bed. From his window and the open door, during the summer, he has a view of the back meadow that ends in a gradual slope at the Vistula River, which is bordered by poplar trees and weeping willows. People, who come to bring their shoes to be fixed or to order new ones to be made, are never in a hurry to leave. The raucous laughter from the cobbler shop reverberates throughout the house. My sanguine father balances the serious, hardworking, no-nonsense personality of my mother.

One of the chores I sometimes share with my sister Paula is taking our cows to a variety of grazing grounds, all of them unfenced. With a switch close by, I revel in the pungent grass, reading, dreaming, and talking to my friends who are similarly employed with their herds near-by. Sometimes, Paula and I take turns watching all the cows while the others have a swim in the river. In the evenings we often roast potatoes in the open fire.

"This idyllic life, at least for me who sees it through the eyes of a seven year old, ends abruptly with the assassination of Arch Duke Ferdinand. The First World War has begun!

As the Russians take over Poland, all the men of our village are loaded into cattle railroad cars and transported to Russia. My father is among them. Several weeks later the same fate awaits our family and that of others in the villages of those of German descent. The farms are confiscated by the enemy. My mother, who is expecting her fifth child, and her three children are allowed to occupy one room of their house until after the birth of the baby. The rest of the dwelling is taken over by the Russian officers who make it their headquarters. Mother is now the Russians' maid. She cooks for them, washes and irons their uniforms, cleans and mends. We have heard nothing from our father. One day I become very ill. The diagnosis—measles. The Russians, scared of catching the disease, leave. For two weeks peace descends on our household. Shortly after the return of the officers, the baby is born with the help of a midwife. Meanwhile, the fighting front has advanced to fourteen kilometers of our village. We can hear the canon fire rattling our windows. When baby Olga reaches the sixth week of life, we are loaded onto horse drawn wagons, and with armed soldiers marching on each side of us, we are taken to Warsaw. It turns out to be a long, slow trek on unpaved, dusty roads which become treacherous when it starts to rain. The three of us huddle close to mother, who is doing her best to protect the baby from the downpour. Paula and I try our best to comfort three-year-old Eduard. When we finally reach the capital we are housed two nights in a women's prison. From there we are taken to the train that bears us to Russia. After a three day and three night journey we arrive in Kharkov and are ordered to disembark. Bewildered we view our surroundings. There are several other refugee families on the train platform, also looking confused. My mother has hoarded a piece of gold which she brought with us. Together with another family, we locate an apartment to rent. We take turns cooking the meager meals on the wood stove in the kitchen. The bare floor is our bed except for the baby who sleeps on a pillow. It has been six months since we have seen our father.

"The money received from selling the gold piece is coming to an end. My mother speaks no Russian. Paula and I, however, are learning it fast as we play outside with the neighborhood children. When things start to look the darkest, our father appears on our doorstep. He has learned of our whereabouts from one of the refugee families who was on our train. The three of us are eager to introduce him to our baby sister, whom he gently cradles in his arms. He sets up a shoe repair shop in our apartment as soon as the other family moves out. Paula reluctantly helps him with the repairs. She feels that this is not a woman's job and runs from the room every time a customer shows up.

"We gather wood for our cooking in the forest nearby and haul water in buckets hung from a yoke across our shoulders from a well three kilometers from where we live. In the spring, my mother plants a garden. Because potatoes are scarce, she devotes the largest part to them. Slowly we accumulate some things to make our home more comfortable.

"Paula and I attended the local school which is located three kilometers away. During the winter when temperatures sometimes drop to 50 degrees below zero, it is miserable. Our clothes are not adequate for the bitter cold. My legs are frostbitten. I still suffer from this. Our neighbors are kind to us and we make many friends. Then, one day...we hear the sound of canons and of airplanes flying overhead. I am so scared that I hide under the table and recite the

Lord's Prayer as fast as the bullet shells explode. The Germans take the city, and we are told to go back to our own country. We have lived in Kharkov three years. Once again the refugees are loaded into cattle cars and transported to Poland."

****

The card players left the far corner of the room. Mrs. Troper got up from her chair to open the door for the man in the wheel chair. Franz felt stiff from sitting so still and concentrating on the speaker's every word. He walked over to the fire place and stretched his athletic frame. As his narrator came back, she observed: "You've probably heard enough to last you a long time," she teased.

"If you're not too tired, please continue," he begged.

Sitting opposite him once more, she resumed her story, this time in the past tense, Franz noted.

****

"We were so excited to be going home at last that the discomforts of the journey were easily rationalized. However, when the train stopped in the middle of a dense forest and the engine was disconnected, taking off in the opposite direction from where we were headed, our euphoria transformed into panic. There was nothing else to do except to make the best of it. We converted the cattle car which we shared with another family, into a make-shift home that was to serve us for the next three weeks, at which time the locomotive appeared once again to transport us back to Poland.

"It was a long, tiring journey. Now that it was almost over, our spirits were lifted in anticipation. I could hardly wait to swing open the white picket gate and race down the smooth path leading to our own home of which I had such happy memories. Running ahead of everybody, I didn't notice the dilapidation of our homesteads. My full attention was fixed on the stork's nest perched upon the gable of our roof which identified our house. Hampered by the bundles I was carrying I made a dash for it and reached our residence ahead of the others. For a moment I thought I had come to the wrong place. There was no gate, no fence, the path was full of ruts, and the river rocks that outlined it, which I had so carefully painted, were nowhere to be seen. The bushes and flowers were trampled, and to top it all off, there was light shining through the windows. I was brought back to reality when I heard the sobs of my mother behind me. Given a gentle push from behind, I stumbled forward. A heavyset blond woman met us in the hallway. There was no welcoming smile in her cold blue eyes. My father who spoke Polish wanted to know what she was doing in our house. Brazenly she informed him that it was hers now since she had bought it. Father told her in no uncertain terms that we were not going away. In the end, she agreed to let us have one of the rooms to live in until we made other arrangements.

"We lived six months with this disagreeable family. It took that long to prove that they had not bought the house. When they finally left, my parents began the daunting process of restoring our property to its original state."

The rain had stopped sometime in the afternoon but Franz hadn't noticed when. He said good-bye to this diminutive woman; he guessed that she was no taller than five foot two inches. She insisted that he call her by her given name: Martha. "You know more about our family than most people; therefore, let us not be so formal," she suggested. Franz agreed.

Walking to his car, Franz was surprised to see the lights twinkling below, competing with those in the sky. Shifting the car into low gear, he descended the hill. There was so much to think about, so much to sort out and store in his mind. He was gripped by what he had heard and marveled at the resilience of the human spirit when it was bolstered by faith. He was determined more than ever to renew his efforts to obtain permission to visit Paul and Margaret.

THIRTEEN

Martha didn't switch on the light as she entered her room. Through the window the light of the stars and the moon transported her to the world that she had recreated for the sympathetic listener. She didn't realize how exhausting this had been. The shadowy outline of the pine trees changed into poplars standing at attention descending to the river below.

****

"Take off your apron, Martha, company is coming up the path. Oh look, it's Rev. Schultz, and he has a handsome stranger with him."

"Stop gawking, Olga, and get away from the window."

"Well, what do you think, Martha; is he good looking or not?"

"I never considered Rev. Schultz to be that handsome."

"Stop teasing, you know whom I mean."

"How does that poem go, 'my heart leaps up when I behold a stranger, dark and tall'?"

"Hardly, but go on, maybe you can improve on that English poet." With that remark, Martha hung her apron on the nail near the stove and shoved the broom she had been using into a corner. She smoothed back a strand of dark brown hair from her forehead and listened to the sound of Father's jovial greeting penetrating into the kitchen.

"Albertine is visiting a sick neighbor but Martha and Olga will fix you something to eat. We're honored to have you stay the night, or as many as you want. You know our home is always open to our friends and their guests. Go right into the kitchen," she heard her father say.

"Thank you, Mr. Meister; we appreciate your hospitality."

The door opened, the strangers walked in, and to Martha, the tall, dark one would never be a stranger again.

****

A slight shiver shook her frame and brought her back to the present. She switched on the light and prepared for bed. Snuggling under the covers she tried in vain to stop her mind from racing, descending into the half-forgotten past. What had triggered the memories of Jacob? She wondered, was it the wavy dark hair and expressive brown eyes of the Swiss? On the brink of sleep her eyes followed a falling star, falling, falling—burning out, becoming one with the earth.

"What did these people want of her? Why were they in her room? Why was that black dress, hat and stockings lying on the bed? Muffled voices urged her to do something, what was it? Gentle hands reached out toward her from all directions. Something was pulled over her head. Something soft but restrictive was pushing her hair onto her forehead. The veil was obstructing her view. She reached to push it away but found that her hands were grasping a cob web that threatened to entangle her whole being. There were more hands— hands grasping her elbows and exerting gentle pressure, urging her into motion. Frantically she searched the room for her children only to see them being led away by strangers. They were dressed in black—she never dressed her children in black! Tears stung her cheeks —she never dressed her children in black! Doors closed, doors opened, she felt herself floating past houses and shops and flower stands. Flowers were everywhere. The scent was overpowering— people—and more people—all looking at her! Eyes fastened on her— sad, liquid—pain filled. On both sides patient hands directed her through the throng towards a rectangular shape elevated, encased by wreaths. Through a clouded mist she saw him peacefully asleep on white satin pillows, graceful long fingers entwined, wavy dark hair carefully combed—resting, sleeping. She felt herself falling, hands outstretched toward him —falling—falling! A heart wrenching cry woke her. With one bound she sat upright in bed releasing her grip from the sheets—touching the wet pillow—starring into the dark.

She lay awake a long time. Impression upon impression crowded in upon her. She was home once more. She was wearing an apron, negotiating a ladder leaning against a cherry tree in her parent's orchard, shouting to her sister who was filling her basket with the fragrant fruit. At regular intervals she stuffed a handful of cherries into her mouth and expelled the pits in a shower that pinged against the metal pail at the foot of the tree. The scene switched to Kharkov. She was a school girl fascinated by a local boy inserting a handful of sunflower seeds into his mouth and ejecting the hulls from both corners of his mouth. The redundant ping grew louder as the machine gun bullets hit the metal train cars, penetrating the open windows, shattering the closed ones.

She saw herself as a teen in the company of her peers, musical instruments and Bibles in their hands, walking along the unpaved roads, taking shortcuts through meadows and woods on the way to a youth gathering at a neighboring village. Paula had taught herself to play the mandolin. The haunting tunes she plucked out of the instrument could bring forth tears from anyone listening to her. The young people sang, played their instruments, and studied God's Word. Walking back arm in arm, they made their way home as shadows lengthened and the air grew chilly. It was this joy and deep found faith that had sustained her through "the valley of the shadow of death."

She relived the excitement of an all-night cook-out making syrup from sugar beets. Several neighbors got together for this. They prepared the vegetables to be put into large iron vats and cooked down on an open fire in their back yard. There was singing, talking, gossiping and flirting, by the young of course, as delicious food was consumed and washed down with apple cider or tea. The older people reminisced about their experiences in Russia and the hard times of building up what had been destroyed during the refugee years. She remembered how disturbed her mother was when she had come back from talking to their pastor about the price for her confirmation. This rite was so important to the parents that in the end they borrowed money for a proper dress and the fee to participate in this religious ceremony their church required. Borrowing money was not practiced by the Meister family, who would rather do without than ask others for help. Consequently, when the church showed no consideration for their impoverished condition, it lost some of the power it had held over them. When, a little later, visiting pastors and missionaries came to their village proclaiming a Gospel of mercy and grace, they were ready to listen. She, Martha, was the first one in their family to respond to the claims of the Gospel. She had never felt herself good or strong enough to live a righteous life which God required from those who called Him their Father. So when it was shown to her from the Bible that God's Son, Jesus, had come to earth to live that righteous life, die for her sins, and through His substitutionary death and resurrection declare those holy who believed God, she joyfully accepted this truth. Each family member responded differently to the message. It was hard to change a life-long belief taught by their church—salvation by works— to salvation by grace. However, in the end, by observing the joy and freedom in Martha's life, they too believed. This had unhappy consequences. The church responded with persecution, which proved to be counterproductive because it resulted in an explosion of converts who met for worship in the Meister's home. A long line of visiting pastors, missionaries and evangelists from different parts of the world passed through their home and enjoyed their hospitality. Most of these were now a fading memory, except for one, the one who came with Pastor Schultz. The latter had introduced him as Jacob who was a missionary to the Jews in Warsaw. He was supported by an organization from England, called Mildmay Mission. This serious young man impressed Martha as deeply caring and sincere. She sensed that he had won his conviction out of infinite pain. Her light-hearted, extraverted nature attracted her to this man who lived in a different dimension than she. She was not the only one who felt that way about him. The young people who heard him share his experiences from his work as a missionary were deeply stirred by his passion for the lost. They wanted to hear more. He was invited to come back. It was soon apparent that Jacob's frequent visits were motivated by more than leading Bible studies. It wasn't easy to be alone with Martha. Her brother and sisters couldn't see why he preferred her company to theirs. They tagged along on walks and joined them when they went for a swim in the river. Once he even had to buy time alone with her by bribing Olga to go and pick berries. Their courtship was drawn out to two years. The trip from Warsaw to Gorzewnica was exhausting and time consuming, time that Jacob could ill afford. Her family and friends pointed out how difficult life would be for her in a big city, subsisting on a small salary, living among strangers without the support of parents-in-law. The latter were not in favor of Jacob's choice of a wife. However, nothing could dissuade the young couple from becoming one. On October 28, 1933, the wedding took place in her parents' home. A new adventure began.

FOURTEEN

Franz re-read the letter his mother handed him when he returned from work.

Dear Uncle Franz,

"Today, something wonderful happened. I was the good fairy in a play. The one about a fisherman who is granted three wishes and he wastes them all because he doesn't think first. He comes home from fishing and tells his wife that he had caught a great fish that started talking to him, begging him to let it go. The man is so startled to hear a fish talking that he lets it go free. When he comes home and tells his wife about it, she doesn't leave him in peace until he goes back and gets a promise from this magic fish to grant him three wishes. The fish agrees. The couple is so happy because now they can become rich and live in luxury. But the man is hungry and without thinking says: "I wish I had a nice fat sausage in front of me right now." Of course, the sausage appears on a plate before him. His wife is furious, so they start arguing until the man gets so exasperated that he says: "I wish this sausage was right on your nose." This happens. You guessed what the third wish was. So the couple isn't better off than they were before, and therefore have to learn how to make the best of it. Well, in our reading class we changed the story a little so that the wishes are granted by a fairy instead of a fish. Then we acted it out before the rest of the class. Our teacher was so pleased with us that she decided we would present it to the rest of the Kinderheim. We made costumes and mine was the most beautiful. I wish you could have seen it. Paul liked the part best when I attached the sausage to the woman's nose. He said that if he had made the last wish, the woman would still walk around with her long nose to remind her that she shouldn't argue so much.

"Mother wrote that you visited her on Sunday. I'm glad you did that. I hope and pray that you will someday visit us too. We have so much to show you."

Franz knew that he must exert more pressure on the director of the Kinderheim Morgenlicht to allow him to see the children. When he finally obtained permission to do so, he wasted no time in doing just that.

He checked into the Gasthaus zum Loewen in Trogen on Saturday noon. After a quick lunch, he drove the few kilometers in the direction that was pointed out to him. He found the two-storied chalet type house located close to the road, surrounded on two sides by trees and a meadow, and a drop-off on the other side. As he approached the house, he heard children's voices coming from the meadow in the rear of the Heim. Resisting the urge to go looking for Paul and Margaret, he proceeded to the entrance. He was met by someone who conducted him to the director's office. Dr. Wasserman received him cordially, but in a cool manner pointing out that she didn't like to make exceptions to the "no visiting" rule. She meticulously explained to him that it only led to homesickness on the children's part. However, since he had been so persistent, she was allowing him to see the two just this time. After getting her grudging permission to take the children off campus on Sunday, he thankfully left her presence. Rounding the corner of the building he stood for a moment in the shelter of the wisteria trellis. It was a perfect vantage point to observe the children's activities without being seen. There it was, just as Margaret had described it. The meadow dominated by a grandfather oak with a bench built around it. And there sitting on the bench reading a book, sat Margaret. She was completely oblivious to the shouting ball playing children in her vicinity. It took a moment to distinguish Paul from the rest of the noisy group. He was holding the ball, running full speed ahead toward the opposite side of the field, being pursued by a bunch of screaming youngsters. Franz breathed a sigh of relief when he saw that the boy had made it safely home without being tagged. The field was now clear between him and the diminutive figure under the oak tree. A few long strides brought him to the bench on which he sat down. He marveled at the total concentration when she didn't look up.

"That must be one fascinating story," he ventured.

The book slid to the ground. The eyes fastened on him were wide with surprise and disbelief. Her lips moved without a sound.

"So I take it that Dr. Wasserman didn't tell you that I was coming today? Are you disappointed?"

"Disappointed? Oh, Uncle Franz, tell me I'm not dreaming, that it's really you sitting on this bench!"

"Well, unless you have conjured me up, you lovely fairy, then it's really me—Franz Vogel at your service."

"Oh, stop playing games, it is really you! Oh, I am so glad that God answered our prayers!"

Before he could say another word, she was off like a deer. She reached Paul's side and then both raced towards him. A cannon ball almost knocked him off his seat as a tangle of legs and arms landed on his knees and a sweaty little face pressed against his. A hundred questions assailed him in rapid succession.

"How did you come here? Did you take the train? Did you come by car? How fast did you drive? How long are you staying? Can you take us for a fast car ride? You did come by car, didn't you?"

"Which question do you want me to answer first?" Franz chuckled.

"Oh, how long can you stay, Uncle Franz? I think that's the most important one, don't you, Paul?"

"You both know that this is not vacation time either for me or for you; therefore, I have to be back at work on Monday morning."

"That's not half long enough, but did you bring your car?" Paul stomped from one foot to the other in front of Franz.

"Yes, Paul, I came by car, and we'll go for a long ride on Sunday; does that please you?"

"That will be terrific!"

"Uncle Franz, do you want us to show you around a bit?" Margaret interjected shyly.

"I'd enjoy that! I almost feel as if I've been here before because you have made me see it in your letters, Margaret."

"Wait here, please, I'll have to tell Tante Doris where we are going." And with that, Margaret's lithe figure disappeared into the house.

"She said that it's okay, but we are not to miss supper at 6 p.m., and you are to eat with us, Uncle Franz."

The next moment he felt a familiar hand being thrust into his, and the other one hesitantly taken as they began to descend the steep ravine in the direction of the creek. The uneven path led through trees and bushes forcing them to walk in single file.

"Doesn't this remind you of Adliswil? Only there the river was wider and there was a real path on each side. At least I pretend that it's there and that you are with us whenever we go for a walk down here," commented Margaret.

"Yes, it is a little like our river, but today we don't need to pretend anything; we can just enjoy the day the way it really is."

"Here are our golden buttercups, Uncle Franz, and there are the forget-me-nots; and look at that bird's nest in the branch of that Linden tree!" Margaret pointed to each object as she spoke excitedly.

The children had so many things to show him as they happily walked along the rippling brook under the cool of the leaf canopy overhead. Presently, they clambered up the bank and made their way back through the meadow. There was just enough time for washing up before the supper bell rang.

He sat between the two at one of the long tables. Miss Doris Fülleman presided at theirs while Dr. Wasserman was seated at the head of the other one. Margaret introduced him to Miss Doris, who appeared to be a sensible young woman. Her kind eyes, behind the spectacles, and the braided crown on her head gave her a schoolmarm's appearance, Franz thought. He noticed that Margaret and she had a mutual respect and appreciation for each other. After the children finished clearing the tables, the three went outside to the bench under the oak where they talked in private before he left for the Gasthaus in Trogen.

At nine the next morning, as promised, he pulled up in front of the Kinderheim where the children eagerly awaited him. Paul, as usual, was interested in the mechanics of driving and at naming the makes of cars they were meeting. Margaret quietly looked out at the scenery, making comments from time to time about something that appeared striking to her.

The previous evening Franz had shown them on the map where Appenzel was located, the town to which they were now heading. They had read in their history book about its unique voting practice, where the men of the town gathered in the main square, dressed in traditional costumes worn hundreds of years ago, and carrying their swords on their belts. The vote was taken audibly and women were not allowed to participate. Franz didn't think that there would be a meeting going on, but he hoped to stimulate their interest in the Swiss democratic practices. Also, there stood a fountain in the town square with a statue of one of the representative voters which he wanted them to see. Besides that, the town itself was very picturesque with houses displaying painted window shutters and several, including the church, had frescos on their walls. The children were impressed. They enjoyed walking along the narrow sidewalks, looking at shop windows displaying elaborate wood carvings.

They ate lunch in a restaurant courtyard profusely decorated with red geraniums and watched the tourists passing by aiming their cameras in every direction. During the dessert, Franz gave them a choice of either staying in Appenzel for the afternoon, or driving to St. Gallen to look at a beautiful baroque cathedral and its world famous abbey library. Both voted for the latter. If he had hoped to impress them, he was gratified beyond expectations. They craned their necks in order to see every detail of the paintings on the vaulted ceiling. Margaret was delighted by the turquoise filigree on top of the capitals of the Corinthian columns, while Paul was drawn to the ornately decorated altar. The library, although very different, was equally astonishing. The warm wood hues of the walls and floors complemented the multicolored leather bound books stacked to the ceiling, which was triple vaulted and decorated with pictures. The inlaid floor with its kaleidoscope pattern was protected from scuffing shoe marks by all visitors being given felt slippers to wear over their shoes. Paul enjoyed himself by sliding along from one end of the room to the other, while the other two examined the cupids stationed half way up the bookcases, representing different occupations current during the time of the building of the Abbey. After buying post cards of what they had seen, they sauntered through the pedestrian shopping zone buying ice cream cones from the street vendors. Franz pointed out typical lace articles in the shop windows for which St. Gallen was famous. All too soon the time came when Franz had to return the children to the Kinderheim and start his long drive home. As he had done previously, to soften the bittersweet pain of farewell, he handed them each a lovely wrapped package and instructed them to hide it under their pillow until the following evening.

A few days after returning from his visit to the Kinderheim in Trogen, he wrote their mother:

"Finally I obtained permission to visit your children. I spent a glorious day and a half with them. They both look suntanned and healthy from being in the fresh air a lot, and eating well balanced meals. Dr. Wasserman kept my visit as a surprise, so you can imagine how taken aback the children were when they first discovered my presence. They showed me their favorite places and introduced me to their best loved teacher, Miss Fülleman. I was told by her that it took Margaret a relatively long time to adjust, and that she still prefers reading to playing with other children.

"Although the children are lacking nothing physically, I would continue if I were you, to apply some pressure to the welfare society to find a home for them near you.

"Oh, yes, we went for a nice drive, to Paul's delight, to Appenzel and St. Gallen, where the two were impressed with Swiss history and the baroque Cathedral and library."

****

At the end of the summer Martha was summoned to the refugee welfare office where she learned of a Karl Gerber family living in Münsingen, near Bern, who was willing to take both children into their home. They had one daughter younger than Paul. Mr. Gerber was a representative for the Elna sewing machines. Mrs. Gerber was a religious woman who promised to take the children to church. Martha could visit her children on weekends.

FIFTEEN

Each holding a small suitcase, a tag around their necks on which was printed the name of their destination, Paul and Margaret stood forlorn on the train platform. As the train approached, the stationmaster motioned them to board it. He reminded them that he had personally instructed the ticket collector to let them know where they were to change trains, and therefore not to worry but to enjoy the trip. They found seats near the window and marveled at the changing landscape flying by.

"We're changing trains in Zürich," Paul said, "do you suppose that Uncle Franz could be at the platform if it weren't a work day?"

"But it is a work day."

"I know, but just suppose, Margaret!"

"The connecting train leaves in ten minutes, so it would be hardly worthwhile coming all that way to the station for so short a time."

"I know, but I wish I could see him so that I could tell him how much I like the watch he gave me."

"Well, we did write him, so he knows how pleased you are with your very own watch, Paul."

"Margaret, do you wish you had received a watch instead of only a locket?"

"No, I like the necklace, especially since it has an Edelweis in it. Remember the stories Tante Doris told us about the Edelweiss being such a rare flower that grows in crevices of rocks in the snow-covered Alps?"

"Of course, I remember. I also know that many mountain climbers who have tried to pick one of these flowers have fallen to their death."

"I don't want to think about that. I only want to remember how precious and rare and lovely it is and that it grows so high up in the pure Alpine air."

"Here comes the ticket collector now."

"So how are the two world travelers? The next stop is Zürich. When you get off, you make your way to the stairs leading down and under the tracks. Go to the left and look at the numbers by each stair case, and at number 12 you go up and wait for the next train. It will have a plaque on which is printed Bern—that's your train. Have a good trip! By the way, when you get to Münsingen, be sure you stay outside the walls!"

"What walls?" Paul wanted to know.

"You'll find out when you get there!" They heard him chuckling as he walked down the aisle.

The children had no problem finding their platform for departure or on getting on the right train. Now there remained one more transfer in Bern. This they also managed successfully with the help of people who noticed the sign on their chests. As they neared their destination they became quiet, starring out the window, yet seeing nothing. When the first sign announcing Münsingen appeared, they collected their things and made their way to the exit. In seconds the platform was almost empty of people. Coming towards them, they noticed a woman holding a little girl by the hand. She was smiling.

"Hello, I'm Frau Gerber, but to you, I'm Tante Frieda. This is my daughter, Erla. I'm glad you didn't miss any of your train connections." She led the way out of the station to where her bicycle was parked. Taking the suitcases from their hands, she placed them on the luggage rack and secured them with bungee cords. Pushing the bike, she chattered amiably while the three children followed in silence. After a few blocks they came to a long driveway at the end of which was a two-story white stucco house with the name Soldanella written on it in calligraphy script.

"This is our home," Tante Frieda announced as they walked towards it. They entered the cool interior and were shown the room they were to share with Erla. The white walls were decorated with pictures of Alpine flowers and prints of Albert Anker's paintings. The red and white checked bedspreads and frilly doilies on the chest of drawers created a friendly atmosphere. Paul's bed was behind a painted screen of Chinese origin. Paul and Margaret were shown where to put their belongings and told to change into something comfortable before coming downstairs to the kitchen where glasses of cold milk and cookies awaited them. When they had finished their snack, Tante Frieda showed them through the rest of the house, and then they all went to the large vegetable garden located on the side of the house.

"Our potato plants are infested with potato bugs this year. You came just in time to help Erla and me to make an end of these pests so that we will have large healthy potatoes to eat this fall and winter." With that, she handed each of the children an empty tin can and showed them where these bugs liked to hide underneath the leaves. She picked one of the bugs off with her fingers and flicked it into the can, pretending not to notice an expression of revulsion on Margaret's face as she suggested making a contest of who could fill their can first. Paul and Erla gingerly went to work on the project, laughing and joking, while Margaret shivered at the touch of the disgusting insects.

The sun had set when the contents of the cans were disposed of and the children washed up for supper. Mr. Gerber came home for the evening meal and met the two. He told them to call him Vati, like Erla did. After trying to make conversation with them and receiving only monosyllabic answers, he gave up the attempt and retired to his office. It had been a long and strenuous day for the children. Tante Frieda realized this and consequently sent them to bed. Margaret cried herself to sleep while Paul fell asleep as soon as his head hit the pillow.

Mrs. Gerber managed her household in a brisk but kind manner. She was used to hard work and expected others to do the same. Everyone had their chores to do. Besides cooking and cleaning, there were rabbits to feed and their cages to be cleaned. Weeding the garden was a never ending task. From time to time, Tante Frieda took the children on an expedition of picking berries to be made into jams and jellies.

The children learned that the house was named after a delicate, purple flower which was one of the first to appear after the snow melted. They also discovered that the large buildings surrounded by massive walls housed inmates of the largest mental institution in

Switzerland. They remembered the comment of the train conductor. Mr. Gerber was more away from home than he was at Soldanella. His job required much traveling. The children soon became accustomed to his absences and didn't miss him. It was much more peaceful without him. When he was home everything revolved around him. He didn't tolerate lighthearted horse play or teasing. He demanded punctuality, especially at meal times, no matter how inconvenient this might be at times to the rest of the household. The house had to be cleaned and dusted and everything carefully put into its place. However, no matter how meticulously his rules were observed, he always found fault. Margaret especially seemed to strike the wrong cord to his high-strung nerves.

"Why are you holding the teapot at that angle when you pour the tea?" he snapped.

"Should I hold it differently?"

"I want you to learn how to think; answer my question."

"I don't know."

"Well, if you'd be a little more analytical, you'd know that if you held it in any other manner, the steam would burn your hand."

"Did you clean my office like I asked you to, Margaret?" he asked another time.

"Yes, I have."

"I can't find a one Franc piece which was lying on my desk, did you see it?"

"No, I haven't." Margaret tried to hide her tears.

"Come with me to the office." With much effort he pulled the heavy desk away from the wall.

"Look," he beckoned. "What do you see?" There, standing on its edge against the wall was the shiny silver sphere. "I thought you said that you cleaned this room."

Without a word she returned to the dining room where the others were still seated at the table. With eyes lowered, she ate her dessert. She felt Tante Frieda's hand pat her knee reassuringly under the table. No, he was not missed when he was absent. Nevertheless, sometimes, Vati could be very charming and amusing. Martha, who visited every other week-end, only saw his latter side. She had a way of bringing out the best in him.

The children were not the only ones to look forward to her visits. Frau Gerber found in her a good listener and wise counselor. Together they walked along the wooded edge of the town, watching the tree branches moving rhythmically to the baton of the wind, and at their feet the bushes and wild flowers responded with shivers of excitement to the symphonic sounds around them. The children, bored by the grown up's conversations, ran ahead playing one of their own made-up games. After a while they returned to Soldanella for coffee and cake before accompanying Martha to the train station where tearful farewells were inevitable.

In late summer the children were registered for school. It was a frightening experience for Paul and Margaret. They had not had any formal schooling since they left Poland.

Mr. Zulliger, Margaret's teacher, was a thirty-year-old bachelor. His large gray eyes behind rimless glasses expressed compassion as he listened to Frau Gerber's account of his new pupil's history. To him, each child was an individual whose uniqueness he sought to develop. He treated his students with respect and guided them towards learning to respond with all their faculties to what he had to offer them. His firmness was couched in sincerity and gentleness which attracted Margaret to him from the start. She found his manner of presenting the study material both strange and challenging. He explained to his class that they were going to only study biology for a certain period of time before going on to a different subject. "You don't give a man in the desert that is dying of thirst only one drop of water," he explained. True to his word, the students read about their subject, wrote about it, drew pictures and made calculations about it. To the girl's astonishment, she never grew tired of this unusual way of learning.

The Swiss children viewed the new pupils suspiciously. They pronounced their language differently from the way Margaret and Paul did. They had no love for Germans. The girl wasn't good in sports and spent recess in a corner of the playground with her nose stuck in a book. The boy, at least, was trying to learn their games and their dialect. When they laughed at the droll way he spoke their Swiss dialect, he laughed with them and tried saying again the words they wanted him to repeat. Adding to their prejudice, these children lived with the family who had recently moved to Münsingen and nobody knew much about them. The house they had built was different from the others in town, and they did not attend the State Church like most of the people there did.

****

Late evenings at the Gerbers were the best part of the day for Margaret and Paul. Chores and homework completed, the family lingered around the supper table talking about the events of the day. When in a good mood, Frau Gerber could be persuaded to recite one of the epic poems she had learned during her school days. The children hung on every word as she narrated Friedrich Schiller's *Die Freundschaft*. They were captivated by the dramatic unfolding of a friendship between two young men which was tested to the point of death by a tyrant and which endured and conquered his embittered spirit. These spellbinding recitations were followed by the bed-time ritual consisting of reading a chapter from The Pilgrim's Progress, followed by prayer and the singing of a petition for a safe night. Once in bed, Tante Frieda tucked in her fledglings and proffered a teaspoonful of powdered milk—her part of protecting against sickness and restoring the damage of malnutrition. However, the precaution to ensure a peaceful night's sleep was no charm against nightmares perpetrated by the horrors of the war. The sounds of marching boots frequently invaded the children's dreams. Grotesque corpses coming to life reached toward their beds, as sirens screamed through blacked-out streets. The worst torture was the gripping fear of being separated from their mother by the fleeing masses seeking shelter from the falling bombs.

SIXTEEN

Karl Gerber had a penchant for designing and building unusual houses. Most of the labor for the first one was done by him and his wife. The money for the undertaking came from the sale of Frieda's land which she inherited from her parents. A wooden chalet built in Belp was the first project, and as far as Frieda knew, it was to be the house of their dreams where they settled down to domestic bliss. She and Karl were newly married. The building completed, she used her creativity to decorate the home to reflect her individuality. The style of the house blended in with the architecture of the community. It was located on the crest of a hill. A strip of forest lay on the other side of the narrow street that ran to the summit. She was happy. Forgotten were the hours of backbreaking labor, short nights, and petty misunderstandings with Karl that had arisen from his rigid adherence to his objectives and his plans. The idyllic life was, however, short lived. Karl Gerber's parents also resided in Belp. Their small home was to be sacrificed for a road project. What better strategy than to move in with their son and daughter-in-law who had more than enough room for two families. Frieda, of course, was not consulted on this arrangement. It was simply thrust on her by her husband. His parents were head-strong people who made Frieda feel as if they were doing her a favor to let her live with them. Even Karl, whose work as Elna sewing machine salesman required him to be away from home often, eventually tired of this arrangement. A plan for another house already formed in his mind which he was anxious to substantiate.

Soldanella in Münsingen was the result. And, again, his right hand assistant in its erection was his subservient wife. This time, however, he did meet opposition from an unexpected source, his neighbors. The style of the two storied house differed from the standard plan used in the Canton Bern. Its architecture had similarities with that of the white stucco buildings in Wallis. Karl did not care that he was unpopular with his neighbors. The brunt of the critics fell on Frieda, who craved acceptance and a peaceful co-existence. On the other hand, what did hurt Karl's pride were the miscalculations he had made in the design which caused the basement to flood after heavy rains. Disgruntled, he put the house up for sale, forbidding his wife to inform future buyers about the defect. After living in Soldanella only three years, it sold.

In his travels as a salesman, Karl had discovered a picturesque piece of property about 40 kilometers from Belp, near the village of Almendingen. Already he envisioned the house that was to stand there, distinct from any others in the vicinity; it was ahead of its time in design. It was to be a one story structure built from large rough-hewn gray stone, superseded by a red tile roof. The large windows would overlook the meadows and fields which allowed an unobstructed view of the Berner Alps outlined in a semi-circle against the horizon. At the back of the house, facing the high hedge that surrounded the estate of a wealthy family, he imagined the vegetable garden his wife would insist on planting. To the south a major two way highway separated the property from a vast strip of forest stretching several kilometers in length toward the village. The reluctant family moved into an upstairs apartment in the neighboring village of Rubingen, where they were to live while the house was being built. His docile wife, however, proved to have a backbone after all, when she refused to assume the role of a construction worker as she had previously done. Now she had three children to look after and besides, she was worn out from the former two ventures. Her health had also deteriorated from her previous participation.

The project proved to be more costly than Karl had calculated. He had chosen building materials that were not native to the area and therefore had to be brought in from a distance. Also, much of the labor had to be contracted out this time. The locals watched with interest as the house took shape. Their opinion was that it was ugly. Karl dismissed their criticism as ignorance and short sightedness. What concerned him more was from where the money was to come. Happily he came on the idea to move Frieda and the children to Belp to live with his parents while his house was being built.

Mrs. Gerber Sr., a widow in her seventies, tall, with wrinkled pale skin and gray hair, presided over her brood with firmness that bordered on harshness. Not only had her two unmarried children, Bernhard and Rosie, moved in with her, but also her oldest son, Rudy, with his family of five. Her calculating blue eyes and thin compressed lips didn't exactly express hospitality to more persons invading the already bulging house. Nevertheless, an upstairs room was readied for Karl and his family. Paul had to share digs with Bernhard, and Margaret shared the bed with Grandma Gerber. Shortly after the move, the new school term started.

SEVENTEEN

With great trepidation Margaret stood beside her new teacher's desk which stood on the dais. The bold, stern-faced man addressing her had no resemblance to her beloved Mr. Zulliger. Unsmiling, he directed her to a seat near the center of the classroom. His long yellowish teeth and authoritative tone of voice brought back unpleasant memories from the past. Timidly she started down the aisle trying to ignore the stares that followed her every move. The blood pounded in her temples, and she felt a constricting sensation in her chest which threatened to strangle her. Sliding into the desk, she hardly noticed the girl with whom she was to share it. Only when the bell rang for the first recess did she steal a long glance at her companion. There was no way of knowing that Claire Dapozzo was to become a life-long friend.

Claire had reason to empathize with the new girl; recently, she had been in Margaret's place herself. Furthermore, she also was a D. P. even though her claim on Switzerland was more substantial than that of Margaret's. Not only was her mother a native, but she had been born and raised in Belp. It was not her fault that her own community looked on her as a prodigal, an outsider. She had forfeited her right as a privileged Swiss citizen when she followed her heart and married an Italian. The fact that he also was born in Switzerland did nothing to soften the criticism or to facilitate the obtaining of legal papers that would give the family a right to be treated as citizens. The Dapozzo family was living with Claire's maternal grandparents until the authorities decided whether or not to grant them permanent status.

Startled by the shrill recess bell, Margaret glanced sideways to discover Claire smiling shyly at her. Her perfectly formed teeth made Margaret conscious of her overbite about which she was teased repeatedly by her peers.

"Do you want to come to the playground with me?" Claire asked.

"I'd rather stay in the classroom and read."

"We're not allowed to remain here during recess."

"Alright then."

"I know a way down the back stairs through the basement which avoids going past the rowdy boys who wait around to tease the girls."

"What's your name?"

"Claire Dapozzo. I heard that you are from Poland."

"How did you know?"

"There are no secrets in Belp where everyone's business is everyone else's."

"How long have you lived in Belp?"

"We moved in with my grandparents seven months ago."

"Your grandparents are Swiss?"

"Yes, but that doesn't make us more popular because we have lived in France since my mother married."

"Do you like it here?"

"No, I wish we were back in our home in Paris. Our teacher, Mr. Oderbolz, is very strict, and the kids are mean and call me ugly names. There are several girls who are friendly when I meet them outside of school, but when they are with the other kids they pretend I'm not visible. Oh, drads, there goes the bell. Hurry, we want to be the first ones back in class."

The rest of the classes went by in a flash in anticipation of walking home with Claire. Margaret had a hundred questions to ask her new friend. For the first time since leaving her homeland, Margaret felt a glimmer of hope of finding a soul-mate.

Over the following months their friendship deepened. Only with Claire was Margaret able to share the turbulent events that had shaped her life as well as the frustrations stemming from being part of the conglomerate Gerber household. She missed her mother desperately and also her relatives still living in Poland.

At first she had liked Bernhard Gerber, thinking that he might be like Franz. But the illusion soon faded when he volunteered to tutor her in mathematics. He often became impatient with her when she could not follow his explanations, which he thought were very logical. His critical attitude resulted in the exact opposite of what he expected. The sessions were frustrating for both the teacher and the student. Margaret's cold and haughty demeanor infuriated Bernhard who attributed her lack of response to inattention and deliberate resistance to his instruction. She, on the other hand, was intimidated by his high handed manner which reminded her of the way her family had been treated in Poland and Germany. Sensing the discord between the two, Tante Frieda averted further unhappiness by taking over the math tutoring. If mathematics was Margaret's Waterloo, her delight was to read and write poetry. She recorded her inspirations into a black-covered notebook which she hid from everyone except Claire. The verses dealt with her disillusionment of the present world system that deprived human beings of family, friends and homeland. She ragged against the suffering of the innocent, the destruction of beauty and the tearing apart of family. She expressed hurt and despair for the violent deaths of uncles and cousins. Yet shimmering through all of the despair like the light of a star through the fog was the conviction that a Heavenly Father understood and sympathized because He had experienced the same in the death of His Son.

The Dapozzos attended the same church as the Gerbers. Margaret and Claire managed to walk to and from the meetings together. On their way home, ascending slowly the steep hill, they often discussed the sermon that had been preached. Neither of the girls was impressed with the importance given to outward appearance: jewelry was vain, short hair a sign of worldliness, bright colors indicated pride, and low-cut necklines were indecent. Claire had learned from her father that God is more concerned with the attitude of the heart and the actions toward one's neighbors, and Margaret's mother wore pins and necklaces.

From time to time when Mr. Dapozzo was back from his travels as an evangelist, he invited the Troper children to his home. He talked with them about their past and listened sympathetically to what they were willing to share with him. The two were impressed by his personal concern for them and by his deep understanding of what they had gone through during the war. His interest was not surprising when they found out that he too, even to a greater degree, had suffered from the reign of the Nazis. In fact, he had been in a concentration camp where he endured brutal atrocities because he had been a member of the French resistance. And yet, there was something different about him. Instead of being embittered by the wrong done to him, he displayed a spirit of forgiveness. He manifested a Christ-like attitude towards his enemies.

EIGHTEEN

The house in Allmendingen was nearing completion. Half packed boxes and suitcases cluttered the upstairs bedroom in Belp. The uprooting of the tender plants that had recently bonded with the soil was to take place once again. Claire and Margaret said tearful farewells, promising eternal friendship and an imminent reunion. Neither realized that the latter would not take place until 45 years later.

They arrived in Allmendingen towards evening. In awe the children witnessed the sun brushing its lips tenderly against the Blümlisalp, which blushing, wrapped its velvet robe around itself before retiring for the night. Their new domicile could never be entirely graceless after having witnessed the celestial display. It was easy to see why Vati had chosen this spot to fulfill his dream. The inside, however, was still in its embryonic state. It would take a lot of work from the rest of the family before it could be called home. Tante Frieda worked tirelessly with the children, inventing games to make the chores seem like fun. Slowly, the empty shell took on form and substance. The collaborators developed pride in their creative process.

The children looked forward to Sundays, which were observed as a day of rest from everyday menial tasks. After church and the midday meal, the children were free to roam the woods across the street, where they looked for berries and mushrooms. Often they worked to build their secret fort. Margaret preferred lounging on the pine needle carpet, escaping into a dream world through a book.

The summer holidays came to an end much too soon. Once again they must adjust to a new school. This time, the two-room school house was not as intimidating as the large one had been in Belp. Paul's teacher was a beautiful young woman wearing black because she was mourning her recently deceased mother. Margaret's teacher, a kindly elderly man with a twinkle in his blue eyes and a ready smile below his neatly trimmed mustache, welcomed her into his class. The students appeared at first indifferent, slightly curious, but mostly they ignored the new girl and boy. The new girl responded by pretending not to care. Instead of joining the others during recess, she stayed at her desk reading. When her teacher discovered how she spent her free time he urged her to join the others. In time she participated in their games, but never found another Claire.

It was an unusually hot Saturday for September. Languidly, the children hoed between the rows of green beans. Their faces streaked with dirt as the perspiration trickled down their cheeks. Their eyes reflected the misery they felt. One of them complained of a headache, while the others insisted that their backs were breaking. The two older ones taunted Erla for not doing her part. Annoyed by their unremitting bickering, Tante Frieda gave in to their demands to be allowed to cool off in the nearby river. In a flash they stripped off their outer garments and tossed them carelessly on the nearby bushes. Then, racing each other, they dove into the refreshing waters. Basking in the undulating waves, bad tempers were soothed and friendships restored. Paul intercepted a dappled frog from escaping under a rock and chased the frightened Erla with it. Margaret, tired of the childish play, distanced herself from the others. She was anxious to try out her new acquired swimming skills in deeper waters. Near the bank the surface appeared opaque. The reeds and rushes rustled in the gentle breeze inviting dragon flies, their delicate wings shimmering in myriad colors, to land on water lily petals. Enchanted by the scene before her, Margaret floated into the still, unruffled pool. The first tentative strokes pulled her to the center of the cove. Suddenly, she felt something slithery and slimy wrap itself around her leg and pull her beneath the surface of the water. Panic stricken she fought desperately to escape the monstrous grip that threatened to suffocate her. For a moment she succeeded to free herself from the sucking, swirling force and then once again the clammy tentacles grasped at her flesh and pulled her into the watery abyss. She felt a giant hand from above pushing her down until her lungs almost burst. Terror gave impetus to propel her to the top once more. Gasping for air she furiously flailed her arms and kicked with every ounce of strength she still possessed. Then, for the third time, the conquering beast was devouring its victim. Pictures of her mother and brother flashed before her—"Help me, Jesus, I don't want to die," she sobbed.

Paul and Erla had become aware that Margaret was no longer near them. They scanned their surroundings but saw no sign of her. Then, from the corner of his eye Paul caught a glimpse of a white arm disappearing beneath the surface of the water. He shouted for Erla to follow him and both running in the direction of the drowning

Margaret, he yelled to the fisherman on the bank for help. As Paul neared the spot where he had seen the quivering hand, he realized that there was a dramatic drop off. He directed Erla to lie down on the shallow bottom and extend her arm as far as possible. Holding on to her hand, he waded up to his armpits into the murky lagoon. Margaret's arms and head surfaced once more, and this time her brother grasped her hand, and he and Erla pulled her to safety. Regurgitating water and gasping for breath, she lay exhausted on the white pebbles. Disinterested, the fisherman reeled in his line, watching the children's curious games.

At home, Mrs. Gerber's face paled as she listened to Paul and Erla's recounting of what had happened. Everyone agreed that it was best not to tell Mrs. Troper about it. However, somehow she found out and was deeply disturbed. From that day on she was determined to redouble her efforts of finding a place where her children could be near her.

NINETEEN

The little village of Worblaufen, near Ittigen, was not as insignificant as it might appear to casual passersby. It boasted a general store, which not only offered most necessities to its villagers, but at the same time acted as a clearing house for the latest news in the vicinity. Since there was no other business except the sawmill, it attracted customers from every walk of life. Mr. Heinz Heimann was one of its regular patrons. He benefited as much from the store's goods as he did from the friendly exchange of the latest happenings in the lives of his neighbors. He realized, of course, that this information was not free because he, even to a greater extent than the rest of the people, contributed to the news making. The villagers had for decades looked up to his family with personal pride. It was they who were responsible for Worblaufen's existence. As long as anyone could remember, the Heimanns' estate had lent dignity and importance to the village. Their lives had in one way or another interacted with that of the owners. Even though only a few people from the village had set foot into the imposing house in which he lived, little of what went on within was not common knowledge. The kernel of truth picked up by an astute delivery boy or seamstress was soon turned over a hundredfold, exfoliated, polished, ground and concocted beyond recognition to be served up for dinner to the news starved population. It was true that the present owner of the estate provided more intriguing fare than his ancestors. Hadn't he married an outsider, a plebeian, a commoner? The stir he caused was as notorious as World War II and as unforgettable and unforgivable in many people's opinion. Even now, as a man in his seventies, snow white hair crowning an aristocratic head, he could not escape the calculating glances of his peers. He was amused by their petty prejudice and it showed in the twinkle of his keen blue eyes. An outsider would not have been able to distinguish the elderly man clad in coveralls from any other farmer chatting about the weather, crops, or latest headlines in the general store. If children on an errand for their mothers happened to be in the shop when Mr. Heimann was there, they managed to sidle up to him and endure his kindly teasing and playful tousling of their hair for the inevitable reward. Slowly sucking the candy he gave them, they made it last as long as possible.

After a friendly good-bye, Mr. Heimann traced his steps towards home. He could take a shortcut through his orchard to reach his destination, but since it was uphill, he chose the less strenuous but longer route. Following the Main street for several blocks he made a sharp left turn and then took the narrow graveled path between grain fields that led to the graceful black iron gate that marked the entrance to the park-like gardens at the front of the residence. The multistoried perfect proportions of the house, capped by a mansard roof, made it unique from any other building in the neighborhood. Forest-green shutters complemented the delicately pink exterior. The largest portion of the house, named Fischrain, was inhabited by him, his wife and only daughter, Betli, whose thirtieth birthday was soon to be celebrated. The west side of Fichrain faced its own courtyard, not visible from the gardens. In it lived Mrs. Heimann's nephew and his young family. He, with the help of hired men, farmed the Heimanns' estate.

Deep in thought, Heinz Heinmann approached the front door, a satisfied smile playing around his lips as he noticed the industrious bees buzzing around the numerous varieties of flowers. The honey harvest would be plenteous, he observed. His bee keeping hobby afforded him a pleasant diversion. Stepping into the cool hall he heard voices in the kitchen, undoubtedly his wife, Eve, was discussing the lunch menu with Laney, their maid who was Eve's niece. From the music room one of Mozart's piano concertos drifted toward him. His daughter Betli was at the piano. He stopped for a moment to listen and then proceeded to his office, where he faced a stack of correspondence.

Having finished reading and sorting the stack of letters and bills, he was just about to pull out his estate ledger when he heard the dinner bell beckoning him for lunch. Thoughtfully, he proceeded to the dining room where Eve, Betli and Laney were already seated at the table. Heinz glanced at each in turn, a playful smile hovering about his lips. He had anticipated the questioning looks of his companions and wondered how long he could keep them in suspense.

"What is the latest gossip, Heinz?" This comment came from Eve, who was placing a meticulously starched napkin on her lap. Heinz' smile broadened as he asked for the salt and pepper to be passed.

"Well, you did go to the Co-op, didn't you?"

All eyes were fastened on him in expectation. He took a bite of his food, winked at Laney, then said: "Good news, Eve; the price of wheat is higher than last year, and there seems to be a greater demand for honey."

Betli's eyes lit up and her infectious laugh rang through the room. Then, in an attempt at seriousness: "Come, Father, stop teasing and tell us the news circulating among our neighbors today."

"Well, can you believe that we are too old to have two children living with us? Foreigners to boot!"

"You actually heard someone say that?" Eve asked incredulously.

"Not in so many words, but that was the gist of it, ignoring the fact that you, Betli, and Laney are not octogenarians yet." Noticing Eve's furrowed brow and puckered lips Heinz perceived that she was not in on the joke.

"They are right! What were you thinking, Heinz, when you agreed to take a fourteen year old and a twelve year old into our home? Don't you realize how a pair of rowdy children will bring an end to our tranquility?"

"Eve, dear, just think of the good we can do for two human beings ravaged by war. Besides, a little liveliness will be a welcome change." He rose from his chair and headed for his office and to the less controversial ledger books.

Martha could hardly contain her excitement when Sister Anna shared the news with her that the Heimanns were willing to take Margaret and Paul into their home. For three interminable years she had prayed for this moment, and now her prayers were to be answered. Tears of joy rewarded Sister Anna for the impassioned pleas she had made to the Heimanns to give the children a place to live near their mother. She had introduced this subject on subsequent visits to the Fischrain until the couple's resistance to hosting two foreign children had broken down and compassion had won them over to her suggestion. Heinz and Betli, once persuaded, looked forward to their home being enlivened. It had been quiet long enough, they reasoned, and there was plenty of room for a dozen children. Eve, on the other hand, envisioned chaos and an unpleasant change to the life she had enjoyed.

The Meister Family
(Children: Paula, Eduard, Martha)

Martha at her sewing machine

Jacob and Martha Troper

Dean and Margaret Lattin

Paul and Ilse
Troper

Margaret Lattin

Cousins at the Grand Tetons

Hadassa,
Kezia,
Sarai,
and
Elie
Manchester

Jim and Christina Thomas

Brandon and Jacob
Thomas

Dan and Melanie Manchester

~ 104 ~   Phil and Sarah Lattin
Jael, Zac, Ben

TWENTY

The air was crisp and a gentle breeze ruffled the myriad colored leaves of the oaks and aspens lining the grounds of the Asyl Gottesgnad. Martha imagined that the foliage was whispering and dancing, reflecting the joy she felt in her heart. She snuggled deeper into her coat collar as she hastened her step towards the railroad station. The song in her heart ascended to the snow-covered mountains, which broadcasted its echo to the valley below. At long last, in the autumn of 1949, she was going to be near her children once again.

Arriving at the train station, she checked the time table once again. Exactly at the time listed in the schedule the train glided into its berth. Passengers poured forth from various compartments, but there was no sign of the children amidst the hustling crowd. Panic gripped her and her mind began to play tricks on her.

She was once again in Warsaw. Her father had died and she and the children were on their way to the funeral. The taxi to transport them to the train station had arrived late due to heavy traffic. Once at their destination, they had difficulty navigating in the hustle and bustle of people trying to get to their train on time. Hampered by the large flower wreath and suitcases they were carrying, they arrived at the designated platform just as the trains on either side were preparing to depart. She had just time to throw the flower wreath into the train compartment and push Margaret after it when the train set in motion. She never forgot the feeling of utter helplessness and the heart wrenching fear that had gripped her at that moment. Fortunately, the conductor on the other side realized her dilemma and came to her aid. He led her and Paul to the soon departing train and assured her that she would meet Margaret at the first stop.

She had expected her daughter to be traumatized by this experience, but instead, Margaret was unruffled and even thought it an exciting adventure. An officer had been kind to her. He had calmed her fear by explaining that her mother and brother were on the following train and would meet her at the next stop. Angels unawares, Martha thought.

Someone bumped into her and almost knocked her off her feet. With a start she came back to reality.

The platform had emptied; the train whizzed by her and in the distance two small figures appeared carrying ungainly bags and suitcases. They looked defenseless and forlorn—alone in an uncaring world. She rushed toward them and enveloped both in her protective embrace.

The children talked incessantly as they walked along the road to the Asyl Gottesgnad. There was so much that had happened in the interval when they were apart, so many questions to be asked and answered, so much for which to be thankful to their heavenly Father. Saying good-bye to the Gerbers turned out to be bittersweet. The children had grown accustomed to the routines and habits of Swiss culture and values. After being tossed from one country to another, from one venue to the next there was stability and continuity at last in the Gerber household, even though they had moved five times in three years. They had grown attached to Tante Frieda and to Erla and even grew to appreciate Vati. They also had friends in school and church whom they would miss. Boarding a train once again represented a cut off from all they had known in order to face unexplored territory, another frightening journey that held no promise of happiness. These anxieties evaporated now that they were with their mother.

TWENTY-ONE

To the delight of the patients on the wards, Martha introduced the children to her friends. They fawned over them to the embarrassment of the two. The sisters invited them to lunch and peppered them with questions about every subject imaginable. Margaret and Paul sighed with relief when their mother led them to her room. At ease at last, they talked about things that mattered to them. They wanted to know as much as possible about the family with whom they were to live. Martha shared what little she knew about the Heimanns, reassuring them that they were kind Christian people who were looking forward to having them live with them. She tried to deflect their anxiety by describing the house and gardens…but soon realized that words failed to convey the reality of what they needed to discover for themselves.

In the distance the church bells chimed, announcing another hour had passed. It was time to wrap up loose ends and prepare to embrace a new chapter in their lives—a blank page waiting to be filled. The sun was still high above the horizon when the three made their way toward the Fischrain. Slowly they made their way along the winding path leading to the iron gate that stood half open inviting them to enter and explore what lay within. Although the children were nervous, they were overcome with wonder at the opulence which met their eyes. They breathed in deeply the fragrance of the great variety of flowers bordering a manicured lawn that cradled a whimsical fountain murmuring to itself. At the end of the path, shaded by gently swaying tree branches, the imposing house dominated the landscape.

Martha was just about to knock at the door when it was opened by Mr. Heimann. His friendly greeting put the visitors at ease. He invited them to leave their luggage in the hall and directed them to the dining room where Eve and Betli were waiting. Hesitantly the children shook hands with the adults, and answered their questions in the Swiss dialect in which Paul was quite fluent while Margaret still struggled to pronounce some of the longer more difficult words. The Heimanns were impressed to hear their native language spoken by these foreign children. Heinz couldn't resist winking at his wife when he noticed her astonishment. One of her objections to hosting the two was her prejudice against having to talk in High German. Presently the swing door to the kitchen opened and Laney appeared carrying steaming bowls of food that smelled delicious. She was introduced as Eve's niece. Although Martha had been a guest at the Fischrain several times before, the Heimanns never tired of hearing more about her past. Heinz was especially interested in every detail of how she survived the horrors of war and despite them retained a positive attitude. He soon recognized that it was her faith in Christ Jesus that gave her the strength and determination to make choices which led her and her children not only to safety but also to a deeper reliance on the fathomless mercy of their heavenly Father. She had lost her husband, most of her family and earthly possessions, and yet he could not detect any self-pity or blaming of others; instead, there emanated an element of gratitude, a solid conviction that God would bring good out of pain. Heinz hung on every word as the story of the refugees unfolded. He tried to put himself into their situation but soon realized the impossibility of it. From time to time he glanced toward the children, wondering how the re-telling of these horrific experiences was affecting them. Paul seemed oblivious to the conversation or maybe pretended to be. He tucked into the roast beef and mashed potatoes with gusto. Margaret, on the other hand, pecked at the food as her large expressive eyes wandered around the room. She seemed to be fascinated by Eve's bell collection and china in the glass cabinet in the corner of the room. Her face was much too serious for a girl of fourteen. He was convinced more than ever that he had done the right thing when he offered to take the children into their home. The meal ended with an apple charlotte that even brought a tentative smile to Margaret's face. Heinz invited everyone to bow their heads as he thanked the Lord for the meal. Then he led the way out of the dining room through the foyer and out of the front door. There beyond the garden, in the far distance, an impressive phenomenon was taking place—the sun setting on the snow-covered mountains set them aglow with a warm shimmering light. Heinz smiled when he saw awe in the expressions of his guests. After saying good-bye to their mother, the children followed Betli to their garret. Margaret shared her room with Laney while Paul had his quarters next to theirs. The view from their rooms overlooked the gardens and beyond to the Alps. Both rooms were simply but functionally furnished. The colorful curtains and quilts created a warm and cozy atmosphere. The children had just finished putting away their few belongings when Laney appeared at the door. She asked Paul to join her and Margaret in their room. Sitting comfortably on the beds with several pillows at their backs, she made the two feel at ease. Paul and Margaret were fascinated with the resemblance of Laney to the stories of Johanna Spyri which they had read at the Gerber's. Blond, blue eyed, braids crowning her head, she looked like a grown-up Heidi herding her goats to the Alm. Her hearty laugh soon dispelled the nervousness of the two. By the time she tucked them into their beds, they knew that they were going to be happy here.

Laney's day started at six. Quietly, so not to wake Margaret, she dressed and descended the narrow staircase that widened at the third floor. She savored the stillness where she could give her thought free reign. Her first stop was across the courtyard to the barn where her brother was milking the cows. She looked forward to exchanging news with him, especially today when she could satisfy his curiosity about the strangers their uncle and aunt had taken into their home. Laney assured him that they were quiet and polite, not boisterous as his three sons were. He didn't take offence at her assessment of his boys; they took after him he was told often enough. A little liveliness was easily tolerated he reminded her. Besides, the house was so well built that the sound did not carry to the Heimann's part of it. A good thing or the landlord would be looking for another tenant, she retorted. Before he could reply, she grabbed the milk pitcher set aside for her and headed to the hen house to collect the eggs.

She prepared breakfast and set the table for three in the dining room. She and the children were to eat later in the comfortable kitchen; because it was Margaret's and Paul's first day at the

Fischrain, they were allowed to sleep in. Everything was ready for them when they appeared at the kitchen door.

She entertained her charges with stories of her home in a little village up in the mountains. During the spring and summer, she told them, she and her brother led their cows high up into the meadows where the grass was sweet and tender. The cows rewarded them with the best tasting milk from which to make butter and cheese.

Presently, Mr. Heimann's jovial "good morning" put an end to Laney's story telling. He invited Paul and Margaret to accompany him on his rounds of the farm yard at the back of the house where Laney's brother, Horst, was scrubbing the stalls. He became their friend when he placed a kitten into each of their hands. They carried the kittens around as they continued to other parts of the estate. From that moment Paul became Heinz's shadow as he basked in the kindness of the gentle owner of the property. Margaret, on the other hand, was Laney's helper and companion. Betli often joined the two in the kitchen. Her friendly manner dispelled Margaret's shyness. Together they washed and dried the eggs that Laney gathered in the mornings. It was Betli who taught the girl how to lay the table when company was expected. She also lent her books that she had enjoyed and treasured when she was a teen. She often joined the children and Laney for their afternoon snack of bread, cheese and apple cider served on the picnic table in the garden.

Eve's delicate health kept her often confined to her bedroom suite. However, she usually made an effort to join the rest of the household in the evenings around the radio to listen to classical music. Mozart was a special favorite of mother and daughter.

The care-free days came to an end much too soon for the children when school started. A fifteen-minute walk through the meadows took them to the village of Ittigen, where the school was located. With trepidation, the children entered their respective class rooms. To Margaret's great surprise, her teacher was Mr. Zulliger, the father of her favorite teacher in Münsingen, where she lived with the Gerbers. Besides teaching, Mr. Hans Zulliger was a well-known author of books written in the Swiss dialect, which was quite rare since High German was the official language used in church and school.

Although Margaret respected her present teacher, she missed the gentle spirit of the son. What made the school experience almost enjoyable was the friendship of a classmate, Francine, who lived near the Heimanns. The girls took turns walking each other home. From Francine's home, Margaret walked up the hill through an apple orchard to the Fischrain. Francine, on the other hand, had an easy downhill trek to her house. As much as Margaret relished Francine's company, she longed to spend more time with her mother. This wish materialized when school let out for Christmas vacation because Martha had received permission from the administration of the Asyl to allow the children to stay with her during their holidays. However, it proved to be different from what she had envisioned.

As autumn gave way to cold and blustering winter, Margaret suffered from re-occurring sore throats which the doctors diagnosed as tonsillitis. They recommended a tonsillectomy as soon as possible.

And since there was no better time for this than the holidays, an appointment for surgery was made. The night before the operation, Margaret stayed wide awake starring into the dark, imagining horrible things that could go wrong during the coming ordeal. Her mother's reassuring words did little to alleviate the fear that had gripped her. Just as she had imagined it, the nightmare while under the anesthesia came to haunt her. Floating ghouls encircled her, laughing garrulously as they danced to an unearthly beat. Faster and faster they whirled around her until she felt herself floating to the top of the ceiling, and becoming one with them. They called her name and beckoned her to follow them into an abyss opening in front of her. Then their voices became just one. Again and again she heard her name until her eyes opened and she saw a woman in white smiling reassuringly at her.

Safe in her mother's room once again, she enjoyed the attention she received from family and friends. Cards and little gifts came her way, and ice cream was a special treat that made the pain almost go away.

One evening when Martha and Paul were having dinner downstairs in the staff dining room, Margaret was startled by a rumbling noise not unlike that of the bombers she had heard in the past. Suddenly the building shook, the walls threatened to cave in, the sewing machine slid to the edge of the table it was sitting on, and the bed heaved from side to side. Returning to her room, Martha and Paul heard sobbing. When Margaret emerged from under the bed covers, they listened in surprise as she described what she experienced while they were away. All they had felt of the earthquake was a slight stirring of the chairs on which they were sitting. Martha had looked under hers, expecting the dog to be there; that had disturbed her.

Margaret used her time while recuperating from the tonsillectomy to read and also to memorize a long poem in the Swiss dialect which she was asked to recite at the Christmas dinner of the staff and their families. Dressed in a dark blue sailor dress that her mother had sewn for her, she gave a fine performance that delighted her audience. Only Paul claimed to have noticed that she shook in her boots, as he put it.

The holidays ended and the two returned to the Heimanns' residence and to school once more. When the snow melted and delicate crocuses and Soldanellas pushed their heads out of the frozen ground, the children greeted spring with gladness. The wool stockings, caps and gloves were packed away and exchanged for lighter and more comfortable clothes. Walking through the woods with their mother on the weekends was something to look forward to. While Margaret and Paul enjoyed being in Switzerland, Martha was constantly being confronted by immigration to seek another country in which to live.

Her sister Emilia, who had lived in the United States since she was eighteen years old, had been working since the beginning of the war on permission for them to immigrate to the U.S.; but because they were Polish citizens and the quota was so small for Poles, permission had not been granted. Martha dreaded meeting with the officials only to be told that they had no place to go. She prayed to her heavenly Father for wisdom of what to do.

Out of the blue, literally, the answer came. The director of the Mildmay Mission was vacationing in Switzerland. Though the mission had infrequently made contact with Martha, knowing of Martha's whereabouts, the director felt led to contact her. A meeting was arranged at which she was invited to come to London where she and her children could be together once again.

They had enjoyed the hospitality of the Swiss for four years. Margaret and Paul had lived with the Heimanns almost one of these years. Once again relationships had to be severed; all they knew had to be left behind to face the impending unknown.

TWENTY-TW0

The train, the ship, the bus—the journey passed as if in a dream. An address of a boarding house in hand, the three tired passengers arrived in an unfamiliar city, in a country that did not speak their language nor understand their culture. The only thing they were sure of, however, was that their heavenly Father had led them to this place. Their apprehension disappeared when they were met by Rachmiel Frydland, their friend from Poland, who was attending the University in London. He had taken Jacob Troper's place when he died and had been supported by the Mildmay Mission. Because the hour was late, he left after introducing them to the lady who ran the lodging and promised to see them the next day. The landlady showed them to their room and pointed out on their watch what time breakfast would be served. Exhausted from the long day's travel, they soon fell asleep in their unfamiliar surroundings.

When Martha looked out of the window the next morning, all she could see was dense fog threatening to penetrate even into the interior of their dwelling. She woke the children and together they descended the stairs. Half way down they were met by the landlady who, with rather awkward and almost comical signing, gave them to understand that they were to go back to their room and come back later. Although Martha couldn't comprehend the reason for the delay, the three trooped back to their room. In the dim light it looked drab and unappealing. The monochromatic browns of the heavy drapes, bedspreads and overstuffed chairs left much to be desired. The only redeeming feature was the large picture on the wall of King George VI and Queen Elizabeth. Although there was an ample fire place in the room, Martha couldn't see how it could possibly produce heat because an ugly black iron insert stood in the place where the wood should have been. The children needed to put on sweaters, so this was as good as any time to unpack their belongings and stow them into the closet. That task accomplished, the three hesitantly entered the dining room. People were milling around before taking their places at the long tables. The guests smiled and gestured trying to make conversation with them, but it was soon apparent that none spoke German or Polish. Presently breakfast was served. The hostesses placed plates before them with food, unfamiliar and tasteless, as they soon discovered. The kipper that had been re-constituted from its dried condition was barely palatable to those who had been brought up on continental breakfasts. Martha, who wouldn't think of letting anything go to waste, had just choked down the grayish watery fish, and sighed with contentment of the fait accompli, when the hostess approached her with outstretched hand and asked, "more?' Martha had learned a few English phrases before coming to the U.K. Happy that she understood what this lady was saying, she shook her hand and said, "good morning." The lady smiled, took her plate and returned with another portion. It was a long time before Martha said good morning again.

At lunch time, once again, they were told to come later. It was getting embarrassing. Martha had always prided herself on being on time, which she had also ingrained in her children. She couldn't understand why the process was being repeated. Fortunately, Rachmiel showed up in the afternoon and heard all about their dilemma. Checking his watch against theirs, he informed them that England was an hour behind the continent. The four of them had a good laugh and then adjusted the time on their time pieces. Rachmiel also educated them on the English monetary system. Paul was amazed that the least valuable coin was the biggest. He had never seen such a large penny before. "Those work well in your fire place," he was told, "as well as the shillings and half crowns." He demonstrated how to feed that ungainly looking monster in order to get the gas lit to heat the room. It constantly demanded more and more of their change in order to get the chill dispelled from their living quarters. Fortunately the mission had rented an apartment for them, which they were in the process of furnishing. It was located near the mission's headquarters in East London. Rachmiel estimated that it might be ready for them in a week or two. Before he left, he promised to visit as often as his studies permitted.

There were several new faces at tea time. At their table were two clergy from Norway. Both spoke German with varying proficiency. Palmer Skaar from Trondheim took a special interest in the immigrants. He entertained them with conjuring up pictures of people and places of his beloved Norway that kept his audience enthralled, wishing to someday see it for themselves. He talked of deep, blue fiords, crystal clear lakes and sparkling waterfalls. Even though he was busy attending meetings and preparing reports, he set apart time enough to enjoy this family's friendship. The food didn't seem quite so bland when the Norwegians were there conversing with them. It was a sad day when the clerics had to leave for their homeland.

On the evening of that same day, a missionary from Switzerland came to the boarding house. His name was Ernst Kupferschmid. His interest in the Tropers became apparent when he heard the children conversing in his native dialect. From that moment a life-long friendship was forged. While Martha was recuperating from a nasty cold, Ernst took Paul and Margaret on a sightseeing tour of London. They rode on a double-decker bus to Buckingham Palace to watch the changing of the Guard. Paul had to chuckle when he saw the tall bearskin hats of the soldiers. They joined the people who were lined up on both sides of the street leading to the Palace when they heard that Princess Elizabeth was expected to drive by at any moment. As the Rolls Royce passed, the Princess waved at her admirers. Margaret was enchanted by the beautiful Royal; Paul, on the other hand, couldn't say enough about the car.

Because it was a fairly warm and clear day, Ernst led the children through St. James' Park. Leisurely they strolled by the pond, amused by the antics of the ducks and delighted by the great variety of trees and bushes. They could only imagine how lovely it would be once the flowers were in bloom. From that day on, until he left, Ernst took the two on numerous excursions around the city when weather permitted. When he, too, had to go back to his country, the children were once again disappointed. They did promise to write to each other and hoped it would not be the last time they got together.

Shortly after Ernst left, Rachmiel helped the family move into their apartment in Whitechapel near the London Hospital. Their closest neighbors were interns who trained at the facility. Their merry-making at their weekend parties kept their neighbors awake during summer nights when the windows were open. However, this was a small price to pay in exchange for being united as a family once again.

The flat was on the second floor, accessed by outside stairs. Across the paved courtyard, a business man had his office. He needed someone to clean it, and after getting to know his new tenants, he asked Martha to do it. She was thankful for the opportunity to earn some money. Margaret helped her mother every evening to get the man's place in shape. Even Paul had to lend a hand, mostly filling buckets of water and emptying them. While waiting until the floors were scrubbed, he played with the black and white cat that had followed him home one day. Boots had adopted the family and felt very much at home with them, thanks to Paul, who was especially attached to the feline and had begged his mother to let it stay with them.

Martha also had all kinds of jobs at the mission headquarters. Several of the single missionaries lived there and required all manner of services. She cooked for Dr. Dewitz, who was an immigrant from Germany waiting for papers to come through so that his mother could join him in London. He appreciated the home-cooked meals which reminded him of better times in his native land. He often complimented her on her culinary skills and wondered how she could produce such delicious dishes from the limited groceries available at the market. In 1949, everything was still rationed. Each person received only one egg per week. Sugar, flour and tea were all scarce, as were other items of food. The British complained bitterly about the latter. For most foreigners, that was the least lament because they didn't drink their tea nearly as strong as the Brits did.

Martha teased Dewitz that when his mother arrived he would dismiss her as his cook. "No fear," he countered, "my mother is an excellent physician, but cooking is not her strong point."

At meal time, Dewitz, as he preferred to be called, taught his table companions English words and phrases. He also suggested that Paul and Margaret do some serious study of the language. He asked one of the single ladies living at headquarters to give them lessons. She agreed. She was patient, she was friendly, and she was encouraging, but she spoke no other language except English. Nevertheless, the children made progress. They practiced what they learned on two new-found friends who lived nearby. The brothers, Charles and Arthur, were fourteen and twelve, the same ages as Paul and Margaret. The latter carried a dictionary with her wherever she went. There were many laughs, puzzled looks, misunderstandings, even tears occasionally, but as the start of school approached, the children had a reasonable smattering of the language.

The first day of school was always a frightening experience for Margaret and Paul. This time, however, it was even more harrowing than before. It was a much bigger institution than the ones they had gone to before, and it was in a language they barely understood. Miss

Osborne, their missionary English teacher, had given Margaret a book by Grace Livingstone Hill, the author who wrote Christian-based romance novels. She was very popular with teen age girls. They could easily lose themselves in the fantasy of a rich hero falling in love with a poor girl or vice versa. Furthermore, the stories were set in the United States, which was represented as Utopia. Even with the limited vocabulary that Margaret possessed, and aided by her dictionary, she was able to follow the story and be transported into a world of fairy tales.

Armed with her dictionary and one of the novels, she marched into her assigned classroom. During the time that the teacher taught a subject to the large class, Margaret, sitting toward the back of the room, was unobtrusively reading her romance. She justified her action as not being able to understand what was being said. She was able to get away with this for quite some time. One day, however, the biology teacher noticed her inattention and demanded that she put away the book and participate in the lesson being taught. From that day on she gave deference to all the teachers, especially the biology teacher, who won her respect by believing in her ability to follow what he was saying. He made his lesson interesting by interspersing his own experiences among the subject matter that could be difficult at times.

Some of the girls were both curious and fascinated by the new girl. They included her in their games at recess and initiated her into life at school. One girl especially made sure that she belonged. She was a black girl, Marjorie Mc Laughlin, who became her best friend.

The two enjoyed playing tennis together after school. Marjorie also visited her often in her home.

Paul, who had always made friends easily, participated in all the sports and games. He also had Arthur and Charles watching over him. Together they walked home from school and planned to do homework together.

TWENTY-THREE

Every city has its slums, and London is no exception. The west side was where the rich and middle class resided. The east-end was for the immigrants and the not well to do. Jews, Africans, Slavs and others found reasonable rent there.

Mildmay Mission was established as a witness primarily to the Jews. Several meetings during the week took place there. The missionaries reported on the contacts they had made. Prayer and Bible Study were at the center of every gathering. Several of the missionaries were Jewish, but the majority of them were British. Miss Dixon was especially fond of Margaret and Paul. She enjoyed showing the children around the city. She was proud of Westminster Abbey, the Parliament buildings, Covent Garden, and Prince Albert Hall among others. They also strolled through Hyde Park and listened to dissidents airing their grievances on the soap box. At times a fiery preacher tried to sway his audience to his point of view. All this was so new to Paul and Margaret who knew people who had been incarcerated for expressing their opinions that differed with the powers that be.

When David Wetherly came to visit the director of the mission, he was introduced to Martha and her children. He was acquainted with refugees from various countries and was interested to know what had transpired in their lives, listening sympathetically to their stories. When he was in London he often stopped by to visit. He was teased that he liked German and Polish cuisine and therefore couldn't stay away from the widow and her two children. That might have been partially right since he lived alone and had to eat what he prepared. However, his interest in the less fortunate was real and he did what he could to help them both spiritually and financially.

David lived outside a little village in Kent. His house, named Rehoboth, stood all alone, surrounded by fields and woods. It was a beautiful spot, picturesque but also lonely. Several years earlier he had brought his bride to this home, thinking that she would love it as much as he had. However, she found it too out of the way, too far from her neighbors. Since then he had lived in it by himself. However, he was rarely alone. It was grand central station to his immigrant friends, who found the home charming. Several people from the near-by village also came for prayer meetings and fellowship. Now he invited the Troper family for weekends. There they met people with whom they had much in common. They took long walks through the countryside, ate meals where everyone pitched in to make them. They shared their experiences, their hopes for the future and prayed for each other.

****

The Tropers had lived in London for about a year when the mission was given a lovely estate in Harrow to be used as a retreat for missionaries and Christian workers. It was a relatively short distance from London. This location is well known for the famous boys' school, a rival to Eton. Many famous men have attended there, including Winston Churchill and Lord Byron.

The gracious old mansion, by the name of Roselyon, was the perfect setting for contemplation. It was tastefully furnished, if a bit old fashioned, with nooks and crannies for the children to explore and bolster their imagination. The patio in back, accessible by wide French doors, overlooked a well-groomed lawn on which various outdoor games could be played. Trees lining the gently sloping pathway led to an orchard, green houses and vegetable gardens. Overhanging tree branches, bushes, vines and flowers created an atmosphere of quiet seclusion; an oasis for contemplation and the renewing of mind and spirit.

The mission board selected the Bennett family from a list of applicants to be the hosts for this new venture, and Martha was to be their assistant.

Charles and Beth Bennett had much to recommend them for the job. Both were talented musicians. Charles played the violin and Beth the piano. They were friendly, sanguine people who loved the Lord and were well versed in Bible knowledge. They had two children, Christopher, age sixteen and Tina, who was ten years old.

The move from the noisy big city to the quiet countryside was a welcome change for Martha and her children. The Bennetts soon made them feel at home. A large room upstairs was assigned to them for sleeping. Its ceiling was painted to look like the blue sky with white clouds floating in it. Margaret took it as harbinger of heavenly days ahead.

The children soon enjoyed each other's company. Tina, a blue eyed blond and fun-loving bundle of energy, found much to interest her in these expansive surroundings. Christopher, who only allowed his parents to call him by that name, was Chris to everyone else. His temperament resembled that of his mother's. He was tall and slender with brown eyes and hair. He was a deep thinker; — quiet and intelligent— but he also possessed a vibrant sense of humor. He played the piano reasonably well, listened to classical music, enjoyed sports and was at the top of his class at school. He ingeniously discovered a way to rig up a tennis net on the terraced lawn, on which he and Margaret played in their free time. He also introduced her to the music of various composers like Chopin, Schubert, Beethoven, Dvorak and others besides Mozart, who had been her favorite. They discussed the poetry of Keats and Wordsworth and Shelley and wrote some silly verse of their own.

As soon as the establishment was ready for guests, they started arriving. It was soon apparent that more help was needed to accommodate the visitors. An older German lady was hired to be the cook and to assist with other duties wherever needed. Because her name was also Martha, Charles, never at a loss for solving little problems, gave Mrs. Troper the name, *Panni*, the Polish word for Mrs.

Charles, the true extrovert, made sure that entertainment was not lacking. In the evenings everyone gathered in the music room. Charles with his violin and Beth at the piano led the guests in singing, often teaching new choruses and hymns. Parlor games were popular and charades animated even the most reluctant guest. People from different backgrounds and different faiths enjoyed one another's company, and lasting friendships were formed. The children were included in all the merry making as well as in helping with chores and participating in devotions and Bible studies.

School in Harrow was not as terrifying as it had been in the past. Margaret and Paul had learned a fair bit of English in the nineteen months they lived in Great Britain. Their mother still had a tendency to translate directly from German.

One day she took the underground to London. She was planning to be back at Roselyon for dinner. However, when she didn't return until late that evening, her explanation was: "the train moved wrong with me." Everyone had a good laugh at her expense. She, of course, laughed with them.

At school, Margaret found a best friend in Olive. They became inseparable. Olive was often invited to Roselyon. The girls wandered through the extensive gardens of the estate, confiding their secrets to each other, never suspecting that Chris and Paul were hiding behind bushes gathering information with which to tease the girls at unsuspecting moments.

Life at Roselyon was good. The families had settled into a comfortable work routine. They enjoyed each other's company and that of most of the guests. The children were happy and thriving in the fresh country air, giving no thought to the future. Martha, on the other hand, wondered what lay in store for them once they had finished school. Higher education was out of reach for those without means. Only in America was there hope for her two to achieve a University education.

Since the beginning of the war, Martha's sister Emilia and her husband had been trying to obtain permission for Martha and her children to immigrate to the United States. Finally, in December of 1950, the process was completed and the family was allowed to immigrate to America.

When Martha shared this news with Paul and Margaret she was not prepared to meet with such strong objections to leaving all they knew and had come to love for a new beginning, to an unknown and frightening future. There were tears not only from her two, but also from the Bennetts. Patiently she reasoned with the reluctant listeners, laying out the advantages of the move. First and foremost she argued that there was no hope of advancement in their present situation. She had no means to give her children the opportunity for a college education, something she was determined to do. She had experienced, to her bitter disappointment, that war could take away almost everything from individuals except an education.

****

It was an unusual looking group that gathered at the London train station. There was Charles Bennett, with his raucous laugh, who had his fiddle and bow under his arm, Beth, his wife, her perpetual smile, bright as always, and of course, their son Chris, whose serious brown eyes glistened with unshed tears. His sister Tina, a little embarrassed at the attention their group was attracting, stomped impatiently from one foot to the other. Then there was David, who had come all the way from Kent. Several friends from the mission made up the group.

Presently, the gathering, started singing: "God be with you till we meet again," accompanied by the haunting strings of Charles' violin. The instrument which on innumerable occasions had accompanied the piano to Beth's playing Schubert, Chopin, Mozart, as well as hymns and choruses, sounded like a dirge. Margaret's black leather gloves, a farewell present from Chris glistened from the numerous times they touched her cheeks, while Chris' face hid behind a book he had brought along.

The train abruptly pulled away from the platform leaving behind those whom the DP's (displaced persons) had come to love. Away from the land into which they had sunk their roots deep into its soil, sprouting tender shoots to the gentle breeze and warmth of the sun, only to be uprooted once again.

****

It was a foggy day, so typical of the English climate in December, when the train sped towards Southampton. The depressing sound of the fog horn reflected the mood of the three as they boarded the small boat that was to transport them to the French ship, Liberté.

The boat plowed the shallow waters in the drizzling rain, steel-gray waves splashing against its bough. It slowed when the giant ghost-like shape of the Liberté appeared through the yellow fog.

Gathering their belongings the passengers boarded the ship and made their way to their designated cabins. The haunting sound of the ship's horn sent the fluttering sea gulls souring into the air as the engines roared to life, thrusting the vessel forward, putting it out to sea.

Martha, Margaret and Paul were often on deck rather than in their Spartan quarters. Watching the undulating waves driven by the cold wind seemed to calm the churning sensation that threatened to gain the upper hand whenever they were indoors. However, only on days when the sea was especially rough did they miss going to the dining hall. Fortunately, on New Year's Eve, a glassy calmness of the ocean allowed them to fully enjoy the sumptuous banquet the crew had prepared. Later that evening there was dancing, drinking and a ritual to bring in the New Year, 1951, in which they did not participate.

The highlight of the sea crossing was a concert by the Vienna Boys' Choir who were on their way to tour the U.S. Martha encouraged several home-sick boys during the trip. They seemed to appreciate the friendly interest shown to them.

TWENTY-FOUR

On January 2, 1951, the three stood on the deck of the Liberté, and like countless others before them, were overcome with awe as they beheld the colossal lady with the uplifted torch who so poignantly expressed: "Give me your poor, your huddled masses yearning to breathe free....Send these the homeless, tempest-tossed to me..." This described the three perfectly on that cold and dreary day. They were tired of being shuffled from country to country. It didn't take the customs officials long to assess that they were poor. They certainly experienced being huddled together. If they hadn't been homeless and tempest tossed they would not have undertaken this arduous journey. Coming on the Liberté to the land that promised liberty was a good omen: finally there was a place which offered shelter, a refuge to the tempest tossed.

Martha and her 15 year old and 13 year old had to make a conscious effort during the next few days to re-create the feeling of exhilaration that they had experienced on seeing the grand-old lady on the day they arrived. New York City has a tendency to intimidate and crush the spirit of newcomers. The noise of constant traffic, sky-piercing buildings, neon lights and hurrying people can be disorienting and frightening. At the same time, however, those who had been tossed from one place to another had developed a certain amount of tenacity and stubbornness so that they did not allow fear to defeat them. They had come a long way to allow doubt and uncertainty to overwhelm them.

****

There was no one to meet the Tropers. A scrap of paper with an address had been given to Martha by a friend in London which directed them to a boarding house. Once there, they stayed until arrangements were made to take a Greyhound bus to Chicago where Martha's sister Emila was to meet them.

Traveling day and night in a huge bus was a new experience. Glued to the windows in order not to miss a single scene of this new world, the three were astounded by the vastness of the flitting-by landscape. They saw farms scattered here and there, stark against the leaden sky. The homesteads lacked fences outlining the property, so common in Europe. Farm equipment lay scattered, exposed to the elements. Trees appeared black against the snow covered ground. Everything looked bleak and unfamiliar. Only the anticipation of seeing her sister after thirty-eight years prevented Martha from crying. Had she made the right choice to take her children away from what they knew? Was it really God's will to start all over again? As always, she turned her doubts and questions over to her heavenly Father and then concentrated on the view out the window. When the sun began its long slant down the sky and the cold winter night wrapped itself around the landscape, she closed her eyes and tried to picture the upcoming reunion with Emilia.

****

It had been thirty-eight years since she had seen her sister. She was only four years old when Emilia, who was eighteen, went to the United States to seek her fortune. She landed in Chicago working for a well-to-do family. While there, she met Christian Zielke, who had also come from Poland. They married and had two daughters, Martha and Elsie. Chris was a passionate fisherman. When they could afford it, they bought a small house on Blackhawk Island, near Fort Atkinson, Wisconsin, where Chris spent many weekends and holidays fishing on Lake Koshkanang and the Rock River. When he retired, he and Emilia moved to what had been their weekend retreat.

Martha wondered if she would recognize her sister when she saw her after so many years. She pictured her as a tall slender woman, wearing elegant, expensive clothes and high-heeled shoes. She probably wore a fashionable hat trimmed with feathers, like that which Martha had seen in an American magazine. What a surprise, when pulling into the bus station in Chicago she saw out of the bus window a short, rotund lady wearing a scarf on her head. She was accompanied by a tall, good looking man who Martha surmised was her son-in-law. She breathed a sigh of relief realizing that she much preferred this ordinary looking woman to the one she had conjured up in her imagination.

There was no shortage of conversation as Bud drove to the house he shared with his wife and three children in a suburb of Chicago. Emilia and Martha had much catching up to do, while Bud tried to engage the children in small talk. He was amused by their British accent and tried to respond in like manner, prefacing each phrase with "bloody this and bloody that."

The three enjoyed the hospitality of Emilia's family for a few days after which Bud drove them to his mother-in-law's home on Blackhawk Island.

Although the highway had been cleared of snow, the county roads were icy in spots. Snow banks rose on each side of them which made them appear narrower than they really were. Bud had to slow down often for on-coming traffic, barely missing vehicles hogging the road. The nervous passengers were relieved when he pulled into the driveway of the white cottage with the blue roof.

Christian Zielke, who had just returned from ice fishing on Lake Koshkanang, welcomed the travelers into the warm, homey living room. Martha, who had an uncanny knack of discerning peoples' personality at first meeting, judged him to be an indomitable man lacking a sense of humor. His piercing blue eyes and thin compressed lips gave her a clue that this was a man not to be trifled with. He was at least a head taller than his wife, and in contrast to her pleasing plumpness, he was slim.

As the smell of freshly fried fish wafted through the house, Chris bade everyone to the kitchen table and invited them to taste his catch that Emilia had prepared.

There were to be many more delicious meals that the Tropers were to enjoy. But better than the food was getting to know the inhabitants of the home that provided a sense of stability and well-being. The doilies and tablecloths that Emilia crocheted reflected the beauty of the person she was. Chris, who appeared taciturn when the family first arrived, seemed to enjoy their company now. He introduced Margaret and Paul to fishing as well as to the neighborhood. Despite himself, he laughed with Martha who could incorporate humor into most stories she related.

When the school holidays ended, the carefree days for the children also ended. The school bus picked them up early in the mornings and conveyed them to the school in Fort Atkinson where Margaret started as a second semester freshman and Paul as a seventh grader.

The school system was unlike what they had known in England. The students were different as well. They dressed, talked and behaved dissimilarly from their British counterparts. Margaret felt like a misfit. Her hair was braided and worn like a coronet. She didn't own saddle shoes or poodle skirts. Her speech, however, seemed to be what attracted the most attention from her classmates. When her teacher called on her to answer a question, the room became very quiet. All eyes were on her as she stammered: "I don't know."

"Of course you know," the teacher responded. "You answered it correctly on your test."

Many weeks passed and much begging on Margaret's part before her mother consented to her long hair being cut. Eventually she began to blend in with the other girls. However, she never forgot how she first felt about going to school in the U.S.:

"How can I ever forget the dread I had of entering high school in the United States? Somehow it did not fit into my dreams of what life would have in store for me in this new country. Could I have possibly been so naive as to get carried away by the fairytale books of Grace Livingstone Hill which well-meaning Miss Osborne encouraged me to read in order to stimulate my desire to learn English? It certainly had helped in that respect; at the same time, it completely distorted my image of the U.S. This was to be the land where the rich young hero brings perfect happiness to the poor but pure heroin. This picture didn't quite prepare me for the news my mother and aunt brought back from town, along with some old-fashioned cast offs that my brother and I were to wear. To my disappointment, my aunt informed me that the law required one to attend school until one was 16 years old.

"Looking back, I'm surprised that the high school students didn't laugh at the two bewildered kids dressed in outmoded clothes. The British accent with which I spoke their language didn't make me any less interesting to my classmates and more odd to myself. Once they had learned a bit of my background, the curiosity seekers hounded me with questions to which I hadn't the slightest inclination to reply. How could I talk to these happy, faddishly dressed kids who thought it fun to watch a film on World War II? I'm sure now that I had misjudged many of them. There must have been those who truly were interested and would have tried to comprehend at least something that had made their classmate so withdrawn and quiet.

"In spite of my mistrust of being sought only for sensationalism, I made friends. I joined the school newspaper staff and the language clubs. I even won some essay contests, but as a whole, my life in school was lonely. For after all, the stuff for memory building is to a great degree made up of after school activities—parties, dances, prom nights. It didn't take long to circulate the fact to my classmates that I didn't dance. How strange—that they expected me to dance. Where would I have learned? There is no dancing in bomb shelters."

****

As unlikely as she first thought, she liked school. She made lasting friendships and most subjects she studied were fascinating. English was her favorite. Although she struggled with "dissecting" sentences, she loved literature. When the time came to choose what she should study in college, she decided to become an English teacher. Even when Miss Marshall, her teacher, tried to dissuade her from this goal, it only served to make her more determined to pursue this course of study. She later wrote this about how she felt:

"Dear Miss Marshall—she never was able to conceal her true feelings about anything. Had she had the slightest inkling of how far her impulsive opinion would reach, she might have expressed her judgment less devastatingly. Her face registered amusement and astonishment as she spit out sarcastically: "You will never be an English teacher!"

"My biology teacher had casually remarked to my mother how very impassive my face was. He told her that he almost stood on his head to evoke a smile from me, but all in vain. 'Well, I'm certainly not going to laugh at his off-colored jokes,' I remarked to her testily. I was hoping that he was right about my unexpressive face as I tried to absorb the blow just dealt to me by Miss Marshall's honest opinion. Slowly I turned on my heel and went back to my seat. I slipped the returned test paper on Julius Caesar into my notebook. The A+ written in Miss Marshall's hand gave me no pleasure.

"Of course, I reflected later on, she was right. How could she possibly ignore the failing marks on my grammar tests? Maybe I should forget the impossible objective I had set for myself and look at something more easily attainable. Darn that grammar anyway! Why were there so many rules and jargons about a language I had learned by hearing and imitating and which I had little trouble using correctly? Why dissect and tear apart and diagram and put together again a sentence that anyone could say by having heard it numerous times before? Vaguely, I wondered if I had faired any better with my American history teacher had I told him I wanted to follow in his footsteps. But no matter how much I liked that subject it could never have the hold on me as did poetry and prose which transported me into someone else's world, making me forget the reality with which I had to come to terms. The times when I was brought face to face with real life, especially that of the past, the reaction to it must have registered in my face no matter how much I thought I controlled it. I never fooled my civics teacher. Casually he leaned against the wall during the showing of a Second World War film observing the true pathos in the face of one of its real-life victims, and from then on found something else for me to do during the future entertainment of my class mates. Dear Civics teacher, I can't even remember your name anymore—had you only been my English teacher, what worries you could have alleviated."

Margaret enjoyed her extracurricular activities, working on the school newspaper and being active in the Latin and Spanish clubs. Several of the articles she wrote were published in the local newspaper. The one her mother most appreciated was the one entitled "Christmas 1944."

"Christmas had always been a special time of the year for our family even when we were far from our home of Warsaw, Poland.

We were living in the small town of Stühlingen in Germany, not far from the Swiss border. My mother found a small attic apartment to rent that consisted of two rooms divided by a long corridor. Our bedroom was at the far end of the hall from the all-purpose room. During cold winter evenings I dreaded to leave the heated room to pass through the cold passage to the equally cold bedroom. What made this trek bearable was what awaited me in this room—a puffy feather comforter to snuggle under—one of our few possessions we brought with us from Warsaw.

Not only did this comforter provide warmth, but it probably saved my brother's and my life when a bomb exploded near-by, shattering our windows and covering the eiderdown with splinters.

In order to support us, my mother needed work. The only jobs available were in factories that supported the war effort. Because my mother's ankles were frost-bitten in Russia when she was a child during the First World War, she still suffered from open wounds, especially in the winter. Therefore standing all day in a factory was not an option. One of the things my mother had learned as a girl was to sew. Until now she had used that skill only for her family; however, it proved to be a God-send in this situation. She also was good at using the power of persuasion to achieve her ends. And so she ended up sewing soldiers' shirts at our flat. This also made it possible for me and my eight-year-old brother to live at home instead of being sent to a care-center where children were indoctrinated into the glories of the Reich.

And so, Christmas came to Stühlingen as always, but this time to a war-torn village and to a poverty-stricken refugee family from Poland. Christmases have come and gone since then, but this one I have never forgotten.

The store shelves were empty in 1944. There was hardly any food to be had, much less anything that resembled gifts. With tears in her eyes my mother informed us that this Christmas was to be different from any we had experienced before. Because it was war, the Christ child could not bring any gifts as He had in previous years. No matter how earnestly she tried to make us believe this, we couldn't imagine that the Christ child would forget us. So as the season approached, our expectations heightened and mother's knowledge of our impending disappointment must have grieved her more each day.

When we left Poland we could only bring with us what we could carry. However, the doll that my father gave me just before he died was among the things we brought along. Always smiling, unchanged in a world that had become hostile and dangerous, this doll was a link to a sane and happy time that no longer existed for us. In her frilly white dress with blue trim she reminded me of my father's love.

My mother sensed my concern for the doll wearing a summer dress in the dead of winter.

The 25th dawned white and cold. With clenched teeth I threw off my warm feather bed, and then remembered what day it was. I snuggled back into the softness of the comforter as thoughts of suspicion and doubt surfaced into consciousness. Could Mother be right after all? Would there be no Christmas for us this year?

With a sudden bound my feet slapped the cold wooden floor and with a hearty tug at Paul's blanket I raced toward the heated room—Christmas or no, mother would be expecting us for breakfast.

I heard my brother galloping behind me as I threw open the door and then stood as glued to the floor in the middle of the room.

"The Christ child did come, He did. He really did!" I heard Paul's voice beside me as we gaped open-mouthed at a little pine tree on our table. It was decorated with colorful wooden thread spools, paper cut-outs and tiny white candles. And there, sitting beside it was my doll dressed in a woolen plaid cape reaching to her feet with a hood on her blond curls. I had never seen anything more beautiful in all my life! When I finally stopped staring at her I noticed my mother sitting at the sewing machine, her eyes glistening with unshed tears—but there was no time for reflection—my happiness was all-consuming."

TWENTY-FIVE

Meanwhile, Martha found a job working for the local tailor. She rented an apartment near-by that was also within walking distance of the school. The tailor for whom Martha worked was from Austria. He had been in the U.S. for many years, though one could not have judged this by his language proficiency.

Business was rather slow when Martha first came to his shop. This, however, changed once she started to work there. She had always been a perfectionist, and the clientele soon discovered the skill that distinguished her work. She would have enjoyed working for the Austrian if it hadn't been for his drinking habit. This also encouraged his rowdy friends to join him at the shop, until it became one big party at which Martha didn't want to be. So when one of her customers informed her that there was a potential work space for rent upstairs in the J.C. Penny building, she took a daring step and rented the two adjoining rooms. This was not only beneficial for her, but also for Penny's who brought all their alterations to her. This became MARTHA' S TAILOR SHOP and she never lacked for customers.

Paul, as usual, had many friends at school. During the winter months the school set up a ping pong table in the hall. At recess and lunch hour several matches were going on. Paul distinguished himself by being the best player. Outside of school he had a paper route and during the summer he mowed lawns. When he was in high school he worked at the local hospital as an orderly, and also at the swimming pool as a life-guard.

Margaret did most of the house work and cooked the meals that Paul delivered to their mother at the tailor shop. During summer vacations she worked as a nurse's aide at the same hospital as Paul.

When Paul learned to drive a car, the family pooled their money and bought a Volkswagen bug. He drove it to school so that he could go to work right after classes. Often he found the bug on the sidewalk or wedged between two large trees.

On Sundays, the only time Martha's Tailor Shop was closed, Martha prepared the meal her family looked forward to throughout the week. Paul's favorite was chicken soup with homemade noodles. The children loved to watch her do the latter. She cut the dough into unbelievably thin strips which she tossed up several inches into the air and let them float onto the floured breadboard to dry. Margaret, on the other hand, begged for *pirozhki* filled with ground meat, dry cottage cheese or blueberry pie filling.

They had moved from their small first apartment to a ranch style house on Riverside Drive. The slopping lawn at the back of the house ended at the bank of the Rock River. On leisurely evenings or weekend afternoons the family enjoyed sitting on the wooden swing in the back yard, watching the ever changing and yet always the same rippling waters on their way to the far away ocean. This was a favorite place to discuss the happenings of the day or plan for what was to take place on the morrow.

Pastor Bob, the pastor of the church they frequented, encouraged Margaret and Paul to attend camp Cheteck in northern Wisconsin for a week during summer vacation. It became the highlight for the two.

Besides games and swimming, the main emphasis was the teaching of the Word of God. Spiritually gifted pastors and missionaries encouraged campers to live their lives glorifying God. Both Paul and Margaret felt that they wanted to serve the Lord Jesus in some type of Christian ministry.

Martha's dream of providing a higher education for her children was realized when Margaret enrolled at the University of Wisconsin and Paul at Moody Bible Institute in Chicago, Illinois, where he studied to be a pastor.

On several weekends, Margaret took the train to Chicago to visit Paul and the friends she had made while visiting there. One of these excursions she never forgot. She wrote her brother about it:

"Paul, can you believe that your sister spent time in jail? The angry threatening clouds which we expected to dump snow on us in Chicago did exactly that when the train I was on pulled into the station in Janesville, Wisconsin. In fact, there was already snow on the ground from previous storms, so that the roads were impassible for cars. Mother, of course, couldn't possibly drive her VW to come and pick me up. She told me on the phone that she would try her best to find someone who had a heavier vehicle to do so. Meanwhile I made myself as comfortable as possible in the waiting room of the train terminal. Fortunately, I had a book with me. I chatted for a while with the station master, who empathized with my being stranded on a cold winter's night in the inhospitable waiting room. He would be going home soon to a warm supper and the comfort of his family. I assured him that I would be quite alright waiting alone for my ride.

I was completely engrossed in Daphne Du Maurier's REBECCA when the door suddenly opened letting in a cold draft accompanied by a shower of snow flakes and two burly policemen. "Are you Miss Troper," one of them asked. "Please come with us," the other added.

You can imagine what went through my mind at that moment. What have I done? Where are they taking me? How do they know who I am? I was shocked into silence as they ushered me into the back seat of the police car and then completely ignored me. Once at the headquarters they handed me over to the officer on duty and returned to whatever was their next assignment. Providentially, the young man behind the desk had a disarming smile which put me at ease, so that I dared to ask with what I was being charged. He seemed amused at my question and then proceeded to explain that Sergeant Tippton from Fort Atkinson had asked if I could stay there until the roads were cleared so that he could drive me home. I was relieved to hear that, although I wasn't sure how comfortable my sleeping arrangements were going to be in a jail cell. To postpone finding out if the cot I saw beyond the room we were in was as uncomfortable as it looked, I carried on a lengthy conversation with the young officer. He had noticed the book I carried and having read it, we had much to compare and discuss about it. I didn't notice the time, but it must have been long after midnight when Sergeant Tippton walked through the door to convey me home.

Margaret Lattin

You will probably laugh at the awkwardness of this happening to your sister, but all in all it was a lovely weekend with you and your friends at Moody and worth the jail-time experience."

TWENTY-SIX

Martha was also going to school. She attended an evening class to study American history in order to prepare for the exam for becoming a U.S. citizen. It had been five years since they had come to the U.S., which made them eligible to apply for this privilege. Besides learning American history and English in order to pass a test, they needed people to show up at the county court house who would vouch for their good character. Their neighbors were happy to perform that duty. They met all the requirements. Renouncing their Polish citizenship, they had now become Americans.

In 1958, Margaret graduated from the University with a bachelor's degree in Secondary Education. The family celebrated with a trip to Washington D.C. and New England in order to learn more about the country that had offered them a place of belonging. Margaret also wanted to see where some of the authors of American Literature had lived. They visited the homes of Emerson, Thoreau, and Emily Dickenson as well as that of Louise May Alcott among others. They explored the regions where Robert Frost taught and where he wrote his poetry: where Poe and Hawthorne were inspired by Ravens or by the House of Seven Gables. They fell in love with Vermont, New Hampshire, and Massachusetts.

It was providential that Margaret had visited the New England authors' homes and historical places because her first job was to teach junior English which was American Literature. She had only studied English Literature at the University, except for one class in American Lit. Fortunately, there was the summer vacation in which she could bone-up on what awaited her when she signed a contract at a brand new school in Cambria, north of Madison.

****

Nestled among fertile fields of grains and orchards, Cambria was primarily settled by farmers and merchants of Welsh and Dutch origin. A friendly rivalry existed between these two groups, especially among the teens who indulged in name calling, like: "wooden shoes" or "coal diggers."

Margaret soon discovered that there weren't many options of finding a place to live. Fortunately, her principal had suggested checking with a Mrs. Morris who boarded two of his teachers. This lady lived on a quiet tree-shaded street within walking distance of the school. This was important since Margaret had neither a car nor a driver's license.

Mrs. Morris, a diminutive widow, was happy to add a third person to her household. Not only did she provide a pleasant room for each of her boarders, but she also made delicious meals for them.

As the first day of school approached, Margaret wondered if her sophomore and junior English students were as nervous as she.

Arriving early at the school, she printed her name on the black board, the assignment for the following day and a quotation to stimulate their thinking. The latter proved to be a favorite with her students, who often arrived early to see if they could figure out what the author tried to convey. For example: "Life is like a cafeteria; you pick things up as you go along, but in the end you pay in full." A few moments of lively discussion preceded each day's lessons, discussing the quote.

Although Margaret was content with her situation in Cambria, she felt that after being there two years it was time to move on. She realized that unless she used the French she had studied she would soon forget much of it. She started to make inquiries into schools that included foreign languages in their curriculum.

TWENTY-SEVEN

It was at a weekend retreat that Margaret met Dorothea Webster, a social studies teacher from Baraboo, Wisconsin. Dorothea encouraged her to apply to the school board in her town who were looking for a teacher to instruct both junior English and French. As an added incentive, Dorothea praised the beauty of the landscape in and around Baraboo. Devil's Lake was a tourist attraction where people stopped on their way to the Wisconsin Dells, she said. She also offered her a place to stay on the farm where she and her father lived until she found a place in town. Margaret was convinced that this was an answer to prayer. She applied for the position and was accepted. But before beginning her new job, she wanted to fulfill a life-long dream both for her and her family. It was to see Europe once again!

In the summer of 1960, the Tropers boarded an airplane that was to take them back to places and people they hadn't seen since they disembarked the Liberté.

****

The first stop was Paris, France, where they bought a Volkswagen because it was the most economical way for the three to travel. It took all of Paul's concentration to maneuver the vehicle in Paris traffic. They visited museums, parks, art galleries and most of the monuments for which the city was famous before they continued their journey.

The most memorable experience was the reunion with Martha's sister Olga and her children. Because the family lived in East Germany they had come on the pretext of visiting the Zoo in West Berlin. The pass was only good for one day. Martha's family had flown into Berlin to avoid the hassle of going through the communist zone.

The two sisters were ecstatic to be together once again. Martha wanted to know every detail of Olga's escape from Poland into Germany after the war. She also wished to hear more about their mother's death from cancer while in Germany. In the hours that they spent together Martha strongly advised her sister to leave the east zone and move to the west. The only way to do this was to again obtain permission to visit the Zoo for one day. This meant to leave all their worldly possessions behind as well as the two married daughters. Eventually Olga worked up enough courage to take Martha's advice when she and her youngest three children left their home to start all over again in West Germany. She never regretted her decision.

It was with a heavy heart that the sisters and cousins said good-bye to each other and every one returned the way they had come. The Tropers put many miles on their car visiting thirteen countries before returning to the U.S.

****

Margaret taught only one year in Baraboo. It was not that she didn't like it there, but the work-load was too demanding. Not only did she teach several English and French classes, but she also was the Year Book advisor. Correcting papers almost every evening until late at night left little time for recreation or for seeing her mother and brother on weekends.

Through the Department of Education she learned of a progressive French program being offered at the University of Kentucky. Teachers were being taught by native French speakers a new method of language learning called the Audio Lingual Method. Several schools were being equipped with language labs where students could listen to native speakers, and they in turn repeated what they heard. Since teachers had studied the language primarily by translating and writing, this program was to retrain individuals during their summer vacation.

Margaret took the course that made her eligible to teach at a school that had switched to the audio-lingual way of teaching. Racine had a position for a French teacher who was willing to travel to three schools in that town. She accepted the challenge.

The German teacher had the same schedule as she, so they traveled together to each of these schools. Frank had been in the military, stationed in Germany. He had recently returned to the States with a German bride. His language skills were very good and he often practiced them with Margaret during their lunch hour, between schools, overlooking Lake Michigan.

By now Margaret had earned her driver's license and the blue VW bug, which they had bought in Paris, belonged to her. This made it possible to go home on weekends. It was also in Racine where she had rented her first apartment, which she enjoyed despite having to make her own meals.

When the family lived in London they attended a Slavic congregation from time to time. There they met and became friends with Otto and Irma Heit and their daughter Eva. Otto was born in Poland in a part that changed hands between Poland and Germany. Irma was German, a teacher who had been sent to Poland to teach the German children during the war. The two met and married. From England they moved to the U.S. and settled in Milwaukee, Wisconsin, where Eva attended the University.

Now that both families were in the same State, they often got together. Eva and Margaret were the best of friends, enjoying the same books, music and numerous other things.

The Heits lived in a large house in Wauwatosa, a suburb of Milwaukee. It had a spacious backyard boasting a fish pond, and in the attic of their garage, a dovecot.

Every time the families got together, the Heits tried to persuade Margaret to apply for a teaching position near them and live with them. They even took her for a ride to Brookfield, an upper class community where a brand new school had been built. It was tempting!

To please them, she did apply for the position as French teacher, although she never expected to be considered. However, to her surprise, she was summoned to an interview with the school's principal who offered her the job. Although she was reluctant to leave Racine, she was thankful for the opportunity to better her situation.

Meanwhile, Paul was graduating from Moody Bible Institute in Chicago. While studying there he had met George Verwer, who had an exceptional passion for sharing the Gospel. He challenged his fellow students to go with him to Mexico during their school breaks to distribute portions of God's Word and invitations to Bible studies. Paul was one of the volunteers who participated in this venture. On graduating he joined the organization which soon expanded into Europe and other parts of the world under the name of Operation Mobilization or OM.

While at Moody, Paul met a lovely blond by the name of Ilse Turoczy. She spoke German and had a similar background as he. Her father was Hungarian and her mother German. They too had fled their homeland during the war and ended up living in New York City. Ilse had studied dress design and worked in the clothing industry in New York before coming to study in Chicago. She also was interested in joining OM. They married and shortly after went to Europe as missionaries. They were 30 years with this organization before switching to Christar, working primarily with Hindus and Muslims.

TWENTY-EIGHT

Living with the Heits was an ideal situation for Margaret. It was a twenty minute drive to her school. She only had two class preparations to worry about. Because the school had adopted the audio-lingual approach to language learning, there were no papers to correct. This gave her time to interact with Eva and her family.

Ray Brost, the German teacher, also spoke French. At his suggestion, he and Margaret often exchanged classes so that the students heard other accents and expressions. He and his wife invited Margaret to attend concerts and other activities with them. She also had a good relationship with several of the other teachers. She had finally arrived at an ideal place in her life for which she credited her heavenly Father. However, there was an underlying longing for something different. She asked herself if she was really making a difference. What was she doing that a non-believer couldn't do?

One evening she received a telephone call from an acquaintance who informed her that there was an OM all-night prayer meeting at the Emmaus Bible School in Chicago. There were students from the New Tribes Bible Institute who needed a ride to it and could she possibly drive them there. Margaret had never heard of New Tribes, but since she was interested in OM, she agreed to take them there. During the two and a halve hour drive, she learned that NTM focuses on working with primitive indigenous people. First, they make contact with them, and then they learn their language and put it into writing. They then teach the natives to read. The missionaries also translate the Bible in order to present its truths to the people. Moreover, they help these nomadic people to adjust to civilization and instruct them in skills that help them economically.

These students were in the first part of their training. There followed three more years which included boot camp, jungle camp and language school. This was all new to Margaret, and she wanted to learn more about the school and its students.

The drive back was a Herculean effort of staying awake. Her passengers informed her that several of their colleagues were planning to go to Europe with OM in the summer. They invited her to join them on campus where they were having orientation meetings for those interested. She promised to be there.

TWENTY-NINE

It was a cold, blustery evening, the kind on which sane people sit by their fire, wearing their cuddliest slippers, drinking hot chocolate, listening to music. Margaret was tempted to do just that. Instead, she slipped on her winter coat, grabbed her car keys and drove her VW towards NTM Bible Institute. She never suspected that her life was about to change.

Carol, one of the students she had met, waited for her at the front entrance of the imposing building. She conducted her to one of the class rooms where the equipment for the orientation tapes, made by George Verwer, was being set up. Introductions and pleasantries were exchanged. Margaret was seriously considering joining the group going to Europe during her summer vacation. This, however, didn't materialize because she needed the training being offered at the University of Kentucky.

Eva waited up for her when she came home.

"Did you meet a 'prospective one and only,'" she asked?

"Actually, there was a tall, handsome, blue eyed, Californian who may have potential."

"Tell me more; does he have brains?"

"Well, he read Antoine De Saint-Exupery's *Wind Sand and Stars*."

"That definitely makes him potential!"

On subsequent visits to the NTBI Margaret learned more about the auburn haired Californian whose name was Dean Lattin. He was a pilot who soloed on his sixteenth birthday. After earning his A&P license in college, he became a flight instructor in Sacramento. He had been in Switzerland on an exchange program where he learned to land on glaciers. He also flew gliders and sea planes. All these accomplishments were impressive, but most of all was his disarming smile and dedication to share God's Word.

Mrs. Heit invited him and several of his friends to dinner one Sunday where he passed her and Eva's inspection. He was a frequent guest from then on until he left for Europe in the summer of 1963.

Landing in France, he was assigned to a team that provided Christian literature to the OM members who distributed it door to door. He was one of the drivers of a Bedford Van that also carried truck parts, bicycles, and other essentials.

It was late at night when the drivers switched places, and it was Dean's turn to take a break. He crawled into the back of the van and had just fallen asleep when a forcible jolt threw him forward into the spokes of one of the bicycles. Books and equipment flew about the cabin. He heard excited voices talking in French. Extracting himself from the chaos, he emerged into a scene of confusion. Blood streaming from his forehead clouded his vision and the pain in his throbbing ankles increased by the minute. When the ambulance arrived to take the three to the hospital he learned that the driver had fallen asleep and the van had careened into a tree. At the hospital the doctor sewed up his forehead with sixteen stitches. There wasn't much he could do about his sprained ankles. The driver sustained cuts and bruises, but the passenger in the right seat had a broken pelvis. A devastated George Verwer arrived to pray with his crew and to settle the bills incurred. Dean and the driver were released from the hospital after four days, but the one with the broken pelvis had a much longer stay.

The former two were assigned to different teams. Dean's destination was Austria. Was it providential that Paul Troper was the field director in Austria? Was the Lord trying to tell him something? What significance was there to having met Paul's sister? There wasn't time to contemplate any of this. He needed to concentrate on the work that awaited him.

After working three months in France and Austria as a team leader, he returned to Waukesha to continue his studies. He had gained a greater understanding of the need to share the gospel with others. In Europe he and his team had gone door to door offering Christian literature and invitations to Bible studies and to meetings at local churches. They had found indifference on many occasions, but also there were people who were hungry for what they had to offer. The goal of New Tribes Mission was the same as that of OM. However, the methods were completely different. He would find out more once he graduated from Bible School.

****

Paul and Ilse, with their two-year-old daughter Elizabeth, also returned to the U.S. at the end of the summer of 1963. Ilse hadn't been well for quite some time. Because of this they decided to leave

OM for a while until she gained her health back. For two years Paul pastored a church in northern Wisconsin.

From time to time Paul's family visited his mother at the same time that Margaret did. Dean, who had been in contact with Paul in Europe also showed up in Fort Atkinson. —And so the romance began.—

November 22, 1963, is a date no one can ever forget. John Kennedy was assassinated on that day, Paul's daughter Naomi was born, and C.S. Lewis died.

Another date that Dean and Margaret were to remember was August 22, 1964, the day they were married. After a brief honeymoon in Door County, Wisconsin, boot camp awaited them in Fredonia. It wasn't only the NTM training that was rigorous to which they had to adjust, but also to married life. There was a reason why this phase of the training was so named. Those who couldn't adapt to the conditions they were likely to encounter on the mission field were terminated at this point.

A further verification for those remaining in the program was jungle camp. The six weeks experiment was to determine if one could function in primitive conditions. A remote area in northern Wisconsin was chosen as testing grounds.

Having passed the requirements there, Language School followed, where basic linguistics and the trade language of the country in which one was planning to work were taught. For Dean and Margaret it was the Philippines where Tagalog was spoken. The linguistic test that Dean took ranked him capable of language translation. He, however, doubted his ability to be tied to an indoor job requiring hours of sitting at a desk. Although he was willing to do so, he wondered if his education and experience in aviation was being wasted.

What was not being wasted, however, was the time between boot camp and Language School. As the trees burst forth their delicate blossoms and the buttercups displayed their golden heads along the river banks, an even more beautiful sight met the eyes of two adoring parents— a precious baby girl named Christina Diane. It was May; the earth awakened to a new beginning, and so did the inexperienced parents of God's miraculous gift to them. In August, Paul and Ilse were also blessed with another daughter, Lydia.

****

The Christian Service Men's Center in North Chicago needed someone to work there during the summer. They selected Dean and Margaret to fill the vacancy. Baby Christina was more popular than anything else the Center offered to the service men. At the end of summer the couple who were in charge returned and the Lattins headed to Language School.

When Christina was almost two years old, Philip Dean was born in Kenosha. The couple had rented a farm house near the mission's headquarters and the airport where Dean worked primarily as mechanic and flight instructor. Everyone else adored the no-fuss baby boy. Once again it was time to go back to Language School. This time it was even more difficult now that there were two little ones to be taken care of.

When their studies were completed it was time to pack up their belongings and to move in with Martha for a little while until the day of departure for the mission field.

****

The one room apartment on the third floor of the once ostentatious hotel, now the NTM Language Institute, looked like a baggage room of a train station. Boxes, suitcases, duffle bags littered the floor. The smallness of the room, which caused frustration during the year it had been home for two adults and two children, now seemed a blessing. After all, how much stuff can one accumulate in such cramped quarters? Decisively, Margaret placed a poetry book into the box marked "Mission Field". There it was to stay just as surely as the dilapidated doll lying on top of the duffle bag which mysteriously reappeared after Margaret had placed it several times on a pile of things to be given away.

A piercing cry from the hall saved her temporarily from making further decisions as to what was absolutely necessary to take to their field of service. She rushed out of the room to the one-year-old Philip whose sobbing was now somewhat controlled. He had escaped into the long hall bordered by student apartments on each side. The walker he maneuvered had tipped, and he had banged his head on the hard tile floor. His three-year-old sister, Christina, reached him first and tried to console him. Others, who had been attracted by his crying, were on their way back to their rooms, which looked like that of the Lattins, all in different stages of preparation for the big move. Only Fred Kalne remained behind to witness the transformation from the humiliation of inadequacy and helplessness to the healing of the spirit as Philip snuggled into his mother's shoulder.

"Astounding what a mother's touch can do," he commented. "By the way, are you excited about going to the mission field? Just think— three years of preparation have culminated in this moment for which we have longed," he continued.

"We will finally be able to put what we have learned into practice."

Looking past him through the open door of his apartment, Margaret caught sight of Christina playing with his daughter Debbie. The weight on her shoulder of the now relaxed Philip made her change his position. This gave her time to face the underlying fear that needed to be put into words in order to answer Fred's question.

"Frankly, Fred, I'm afraid."

"Afraid? I can almost accept that from anyone else, but not from you. You have lived in so many countries! You understand different cultures and know several languages; what are you afraid of?"

"The one thing that haunts me, Fred, is how are we going to feed our children? We have no churches to support us. I know how it feels to be hungry. I know what it's like to be far from family and friends, and I don't want that for our two."

Doors were opening and closing. People were passing in the hallway, but it didn't' seem to bother Fred. Patiently he reminded her of the principles she ought to have practiced during the three years of training. Had she not found Matthew 6:33 to be true? he asked. This was the time, he reminded her, where head knowledge must be interwoven into the fabric of her life. This was where faith needed to become reality—the time when one had to trust the Lord to supply *all* one's needs, especially as basic as where the next meal would come from.

Yes, she did remember that God promised to dress her as beautifully as He did the lilies of the fields and feed her as He did the sparrows if her priorities were right—putting His kingdom first.

Thirteen years later, at a banquet of a mission school graduating class in Tambo, Bolivia, she heard Fred Kalne share his philosophy of life again. It had not changed from the day he had shared it with her in the hall of the Language School: "If you don't live a miraculous life, you live like any other earthling." She wholeheartedly agreed, for by then she had experienced it herself.

Returning to the apartment the sorting and discarding was interrupted by a knock at the door. Dean was being summoned before the mission committee. This was not a good omen. Margaret awaited his return with trepidation. When he finally returned he actually looked happy. The committee asked him to consider changing his field of service. They desperately needed a pilot to replace the one in Paraguay. Was this what was meant by the saying that: "God will give you the desires of your heart?"

Martha had moved nineteen times during her life; this was to be the last. She had a house built to her specifications—a dream come true—a prayer answered "above and beyond" what she could ask or think.

During the time the four Lattins were with Martha, a friend and her daughter whom Martha knew from Poland came to visit. Dean was gone that weekend helping a friend ferry an airplane from South Dakota to Wisconsin. Martha suggested an excursion to visit a pastor friend of hers. Margaret also knew the family because the Reverent Ernest Rockstad was the inspirational speaker at Camp Cheteck when she and Paul attended there.

After an enjoyable afternoon they started for home. It was beginning to get dark. Margaret was at the wheel of the VW. Martha and Christina were seated next to her; and Tabea, Rosie, and Philip were sitting in the back. On the right, a Pontiac was pulling out from a gas station set back from the highway. Margaret slowed down to allow that car to pull out in front of her. No one could have predicted that the large sedan was going to make a U turn back into the gas station hitting the front left corner of the VW. A piece from the broken windshield cut Margaret's forehead causing rivulets of blood gushing into her eyes, staining her face and the collar of her coat. The people at the gas station brought paper towels and called the ambulance. Tabea and Rosie were taken to one of the hospitals in Madison; Margaret and her family to another. Martha had sustained whip-lash; the children had bumps and bruises.

While the doctor put fourteen stitches into Margaret's forehead, Pastor Rockstad entered the emergency room and prayed with her. The doctors were impressed. Tabea had broken ribs but was soon released. The others were also allowed to go home. Margaret, however, whose pelvis was broken and who had internal injuries, remained two weeks in the hospital.

According to authorities, the driver who caused the accident was drunk. His friends at the gas station wondered how he would make it home.

While recuperating, Margaret still on crutches, the family took the train to visit Dean's family in California. Then it was back to Madison, and from there to Paraguay. The tickets were dated June 9, 1968. The news on the fifth was of Robert Kennedy's murder in Los Angeles.

Martha's tears were not only because of the five year separation from her family but also for the promising young life so senselessly lost.

The plane roared down the runway, lifted laboriously into the air, then banked towards Chicago. Three-year-old Christina waved her hand frantically until she no longer could see her *Oma* (grandmother).

Changing to Braniff in Miami, the seven-and-one-half hour flight to Asuncion, Paraguay, was uneventful.

THIRTY

Stepping off the airplane in Asuncion, the family was unprepared for the penetrating cold that met them. The mission administrator welcomed them warmly, however, as he guided the van through hair-rising traffic to the guest house. He conducted them to the one-room apartment that was to be their home until other accommodations were found.

Several missionaries from the interior, on errands in the capital, were at the guest house. Margaret enjoyed hearing about their experiences on the mission stations. Dean, however, was whisked off to the "aero club" soon after setting foot in Paraguay. The airplane had been out of commission for some time and needed repairs urgently. Often he left for the airport while the children were still asleep and returned after their bedtime.

Pop Heckart, who had served many years with NTM, found a house the Lattins could afford. Like most dwellings it had no provision for heating. The running water was cold only. The cooking facility was a one-burner kerosene camper stove. Dean's first project was to fix a valve and shower head to the bottom of a bucket to be hoisted up on a rope for showers.

It wasn't unusual for cows to wander into the yard and eat the grapefruit off the trees. Margaret was shocked when she discovered that the neighbors kept pigs. One morning Christina came into the kitchen asking, "Mommy, what do I smell? Is it that you didn't take a shower?"

There were no children in the neighborhood that were the children's ages. Christina invented an imaginary friend, called Cheryl. It was always Cheryl who did anything that was naughty. Eventually Cheryl was replaced with a real puppy.

Once a week, Fred Sammons, the administrator at the time, transported all the missionary ladies who were in town to the open air market to do the shopping. "There comes the *gringo* (foreigner) with his harem," the vendors teased.

Once the airplane was in flying condition, the family saw even less of Dean. When the mission committee or language checkers needed to stay in the interior more than one day, Dean also remained with them in order to fly them back when they had completed their work.

There were many lonely days, but memorable ones as well when the missionaries got together for pot-lucks in the courtyard of the guest house. The old-timers reminisced about the good old days when it was tough being a missionary.

When Margaret returned to the States in 1986 for her mother's funeral, she found the following letters among Martha's keepsakes, which described some of the experiences she and her family had.

August 1968

The fog has lifted, approach clearance has been received, the runway is in view, and we are ready for landing. Two months in Paraguay and we are only ready for the approach. How much time does it take to adapt oneself to a culture so foreign to one's own? The first few weeks were spent at the airport to get the Cessna 170 B back into flying condition. Since then many flights have been made which enabled Dean to see most of the mission stations.

One of these flights was to hospitalize an Ayore who had been clawed by a tiger and then shot in the shoulder by one of his friends who was trying to come to his aid. Another flight was to survey an area to relocate the indigenous Ayore people group. Their former location no longer had any water. After this survey, the Ayore and missionaries working with them moved to the new location. Much time, hard work, endless perseverance and prayer have been involved in this move.

A most pleasant surprise for our family was the hop to Filadelfia, a German Mennonite colony. It seemed like a different world from Asuncion. A language barrier no longer existed; the familiar foods were a welcome treat, and best of all, it reminded me so much of my grandparents' home. All, that is, except the snakes and poisonous spiders which are also inhabitants of the *Chaco* (flatlands).

After spending six weeks in the guest house, we finally found a suitable house for rent. It's small and built in the Paraguayan tradition, which to our way of thinking appears a little awkward and inconvenient. It, nevertheless, meets our needs.

Our barrels have not yet arrived, so most of our housekeeping things have been borrowed from our missionaries here. A one-burner kerosene stove has to do for now. A cold shower, which soon will be converted into a bucket shower, constitutes our modern bath. It's amazing how many things one can do without.

June 1969

The annual missionary conference was soon approaching. The plane had to be inspected and put into perfect condition for the busiest flight season of the year. Day after day, Dean returned home exhausted until most the missionaries were flown to the conference grounds. We joined the others, hoping that Dean would at last have a chance to catch up on his needed rest. He blamed the oppressive heat for his lack of energy and loss of appetite. However, the following day all symptoms indicated that he had hepatitis. We had to pack our bags and reluctantly return to the city.

Three months of complete bed rest followed. Finally, after almost four months, Dean is beginning to fly again. The tests still show some abnormality of the liver, and he must be very careful until the analysis proves negative.

Our home responsibilities have increased with the addition of two more members. Philip and Bernie Buchegger have come from the mission station among the Ayore people to live with us so they can attend the Christian Academy in Asuncion.

The highlight of this past year was our visit to Itakyry during the Christmas season. Besides the pleasure of visiting a newly arrived missionary family, we were able to better appreciate the primitive conditions of missionaries working in the interior.

At present we are enjoying cooler "winter" weather. The sudden changes of temperature, however, cause Philip's reoccurring bronchitis.

December 1969

The loud chirp of the locust, the hot North wind, and the oppressive humidity cause the Paraguayans to say: "Ah, Christmas is almost here." We too, have something to mark the coming of the season—to three-year-old Philip, it means that the heavy cast will come off. He fell from a tree and broke his leg. Christina, who is four and a half, looks forward to seeing her little friends whom we are hoping to visit. Dean is looking forward to the flight with his family, for a change, to Yvypyte, and I am anticipating seeing another of our indigenous works.

Dean has spent many hours in the air. Often the weather was treacherous. Frequently the radio did not function. Once it burned a resistor and several transistors and necessitated an emergency landing. The smell of something burning was detected five minutes from the last clearing before a 50 mile stretch of "Green Hell" which presents no possibilities for a touchdown. The clearing on which Dean landed was a miracle. The brush had been cleared only four hours before.

The day after his third birthday, Philip broke the main bone in his lower leg. A heavy cast had to be put on, and he is not allowed to walk until it comes off—two months after the accident. Since he always suffers from severe heat rash during the summer months, we were fearful for him with this added encumbrance. However, the Lord again showed us that He is the Master in all circumstances, for October and November have been unusually cool, for Paraguay, that is. Bronchitis is still a constant threat to him. He has been hospitalized once, and he has taken more antibiotics already than most people take during their lifetime.

Even though the doctor and hospital bills have been many (Dean's four-months' illness of hepatitis), we again experienced the truth of God's promises to supply all our needs. We have been encouraged and even awed at whom God uses to do this. For many of you the sharing of your financial resources is not merely an offering, but a sacrifice. We are grateful to know that you allow the Lord to use you in this manner.

Visiting the Maka Village

There was an air of excitement as we stepped into the small rowboat. The motor began to purr softly and the shore slowly receded. The children squealed with delight as they felt the spray of the Paraguay River on their faces and the warm water with their hands. The ride lasted only ten minutes; and as the boat was moored securely on the sandy beach, we began to climb up the steep banks which were the entrance to the village.

The narrow, winding path through tall swamp grass led us to the rows of scattered mud dwellings of the Maka people. In contrast to these drab dwellings, were the whitewashed, wood buildings with their grass roof, numerous windows and fences. These were the houses where the missionaries had lived. One was now the store and dispensary, the other was occupied by a young indigenous couple, and the third was used for the schoolhouse.

The sight that left a lasting impression with me was found in a typical indigenous dwelling. An elderly woman was sitting on the floor of the hut weaving a "faja" (belt) to be sold to one of the many tourists who visit her village. (These Indigenous people live near the capital city). Her daughter was getting ready to meet one of the tourist boats by putting on the appropriate costume and make-up. In the middle of the hut on a mat, which served as a bed, sat a lovely thirteen-year-old girl. Her shiny black hair fell on her care-stooped shoulders. Her wide sad eyes seemed to be filled with despair.

Why wasn't this girl playing like the other teen-agers, I wondered. Shouldn't she be in school, or at the river swimming, or at least talking with her friends? I found out later from Marv and Dee Cole (the only missionaries working with this group at that time) that this girl had married and her husband had already left her.

How long before the despair in these empty hearts and broken lives will be replaced with the new life that Christ longs to give them? How many more children will crowd a whole lifetime into a mere thirteen years? These indigenous people live so close to civilization, yet they are separated from it by cultural and language differences. They are so accessible to us, but only one missionary family is working with them. There is hope for these people, but too few are willing to share the Gospel with them.

January 1970

Let me tell you about a visit we made with the Buchegger boys to see their parents who are missionaries to the Ayore people. Henry and Joyce had worked with a group of Ayores in Bolivia and learned their language. When the group in Paraguay was contacted, they were asked to come and work with this group.

The night sky of the Chaco was again brilliantly aglow with its countless stars. As they illuminated our path to the indigenous village, we distinguished a group of young men coming toward us. With clubs in hand, yelping dogs running before them, their usually smiling faces seemed grave.

I felt a sudden shudder running up and down my spine as fear of the unknown gripped me. Reassuringly, Joyce turned to us, "Isn't it comforting to know that they are friendly toward us?" I wondered how little it would take to turn their friendliness into hostility.

Being satisfied that we wanted only to visit and sit at their campfire, these guards called off their dogs and accompanied us to their dwellings. The men and boys were sitting in the inner circle, the women on the fire's outer fringes. As my eyes became more accustomed to the semidarkness, I recognized some of the strong young men I had seen in the schoolroom laboriously holding pencils in their hands, who formerly were only accustomed to holding spears and arrows. These brave warriors, most of whom had worn shirts and trousers in the classroom, sat cross-legged on the ground, dust and ashes covering their naked bodies. The older men, smoking their clay pipes, frequently interjected in the animated conversation taking place. I gathered from their grim expressions on their faces and the unusual absence of the young women's teasing, that weighty matters were being discussed.

"I heard the bats tonight," one woman whispered behind me. A grunt of awe was the response of the others. My attention was directed to the main speaker once more and I realized that I hadn't seen him before. Whatever he was saying seemed to agitate the others and to instill fear into the group.

Joyce answered our question about the newcomer and the news that had gripped the others with fear. He and his lady companion had walked from near the Bolivian border, where they had escaped the fate of the rest of their group. Having been away from camp gathering food, they were met on their return by the gruesome sight of their friends' and relatives' heads lying in a circle at their camp site. This killing was the work of the grassland people, Ayores like themselves—their former friends. Should they unite with the group at the Catholic Mission and kill these grassland people before they surprised and massacred them?

The men trustingly turned their questions to Joyce. Others asked, "Do you think they might attack tonight?" "We heard the bats last night," the women added.

"God who watches over our universe also watches over each one of us. We must trust Him," was her answer. For the present this seemed to satisfy them, and their conversation turned to the time when they attacked an unsuspecting Mennonite farm and killed its inhabitants, including the children. "We don't do that anymore," the chief assured Joyce, "for we know that you are our friends now."

On and on they were reminiscing until I could no longer sit in that cramped position, and we left. I wondered how long into the night they would continue their musing. Would they resume the subject of the bats, or commit their fears to the One who could deliver them from their enemies?

May 1971

It's a cold, dreary day. The rain has not let up much since four o'clock yesterday. On the book shelf stands the airplane radio. It had been taken out before the last trip to allow more baggage to be taken along on the flight. The radio has been in the repair shop off and on for four years, but it never has been fixed. I look at it and resent its presence in our house. It's not in its place of service, and therefore it is costing endless hours of concern and anxiety.

I had tuned in on our regular mission radio contact at 5:30 p.m. last night, but due to the bad weather conditions, the transmission was so poor that I couldn't hear anyone on it. However, this morning at 6:30 I heard the following snatches of conversation.

"33 B for 20 L, what is the news on the plane?"

"20 L for 33 B, there are no details—no details!" We know he took off at 4 p.m. last evening and hasn't been heard of since. There was a heavy overcast at that time in Asuncion with rains and thunder storms following an hour later."

The airplane has been missing since its take-off at 4 p.m. yesterday from Yvypyte, our Ava mission work. With a sinking heart I turned off the radio and turned to the clear channel communication from which my only help could come.

Fear thou not; for I am with thee; be not dismayed; for I am thy God:
I will strengthen thee; Yea I will help thee' yea,
I will uphold thee with the
Right hand of my righteousness.
Isaiah 41:10

Dean had just returned from a four-day trip to the various mission stations in the Chaco. He was to spend one day in Asuncion trying to get gas for the airplane then fly to the east side the next day. His passengers were visitors from the States: a couple who teach in one of our mission's training schools. It had taken him practically all day Friday to gas the plane, carting the fuel in five-gallon cans from the main airport to the Air Club of Paraguay where the Cessna is hangered. (The gas situation has been a constant problem since March when the shortage was created to force higher prices.) While he was in the area, he was also to make a survey flight for a map-making company.

The morning was nice and clear although a bit humid. At 3:30 p.m. however, the sky was overcast, and shortly thereafter it began to drizzle. Half an hour later thunder and lightning were followed by heavy rains. The storm had been moving slowly from the north, making radio communications unintelligible. Because of this, I was not able to pick up the Yvypyte station at noon. Consequently, I assumed that the plane's take-off was probably delayed until the next morning.

The morning is wearing on drearily. The trees across the street are veiled in mist. The children are coloring their Sunday school papers. They, as always, have prayed for Daddy's safe return, although they perceived nothing of his present danger. I'm killing time by writing down my emotions and waiting expectantly for a happy conclusion to the story. And again and again the comforting words of the old prophet come into my mind, resulting in a peace deep inside in spite of the restlessness on the surface.

Now, an hour later, I have experienced Romans 8:28 once again in my life. The plane arrived safely at its destination. Through the mist of my tears I saw Dean standing smiling in front of our door. The experience he had, when 20 minutes from Asuncion he realized that he couldn't penetrate the front safely and therefore turned back to find a dry enough airstrip to land, is a story that must wait to be told another time.

In October of 1971, Melanie Grace was born. She weighed less than six lbs. Margaret had been in the hospital during the pregnancy. She had pneumonia. The baby, however, seemed healthy. Her brother and sister couldn't see enough of her. They tiptoed around the crib to see if she was awake so they could talk to her.

Two months later the field committee decided to move the flight program from the capital city to the German Mennonite colony in the Chaco. It was to be located in Filadelfia. Because the Pan-American Highway that went from Asuncion to Bolivia (and passed by Filadelfia) was not paved, traffic came to a stop during the rainy season. The slippery mud trapped vehicles and people for weeks on end anytime between December and April. The airplane was called to the rescue on numerous occasions.

The Lattin family moved into a rented house in January. A new adventure awaited them.

The Chaco is usually dry during the winter season—June to August—but 1972 was considered a drought. Cattle were dropping dead by the thousands. The man-made waterholes had turned to mud in which the cows got stuck because they didn't have the energy to extract themselves from the mire.

The horse-drawn water wagon could be heard rumbling down the streets at any hour, hauling water from the well at the edge of town to the homes whose cisterns had run dry.

The always present dust was hanging thick in the air, and penetrated into the houses covering every object, as the north wind whipped through the colony unleashing its vengeance on everything in its way. Day after day there was no relief from the heat, the dust or the monotony.

October 1972

It was October, the month in which rains can be expected. Dean was working in the hangar on the Cessna 170, which at that time required almost three hours of maintenance for every hour in the air. Suddenly his attention was drawn to the lightning that brightened the horizon. He packed up his tools, locked the hangar door and raced home on the motor bike. He found me sitting in the middle of the driveway, where I had dragged a chair to watch for the coming rain. I wanted it to penetrate every pore of my dehydrated body. Dean, however, had other plans for me. I was to help him clean out our cistern so that it would be a clean vessel to store the precious water. He slid down the rope to the bottom of the cistern. He filled bucket after bucket with filthy slosh that I hauled out by a rope and dumped on the thirsty ground. We were racing against time because already the lightning had intensified and thunder sounded closer.

At midnight our task was completed. Dean was ready to leave the depth. There was one problem we hadn't anticipated. As he shimmied up the rope, he encountered the rope so tightly pressed against the cement neck of the cistern that he couldn't get his fingers around it; and therefore, he couldn't pull himself up any higher. It was too late to ask the neighbors to help. The low porch roof under which the cistern was built did not allow enough space for a ladder to be lowered. For once he was totally dependent on me. I didn't disappoint him. I grabbed him under his arms and proceeded to haul him out of his predicament. I hadn't counted on his being ticklish, however, and my efforts met with peals of laughter and pleas to leave him alone. I didn't want to believe that he was serious about his next suggestion, which was to be pulled out by his hair. In the end, this worked—Dean was safely on terra firma and we met the deadline. Now, let it rain! But rain it didn't!

We put in our order for a few barrels of water which in due time were delivered. Meanwhile, we borrowed pitchers and buckets of water from our neighbor to be used for the most urgent needs.

****

It was a wonderful day for me when I saw the Cessna 206 fly over our house. We were leaving for home leave. This airplane was to replace the ailing 170. The pilot who was replacing us had flown it from the U.S. to Paraguay. Christina, seven and a half, Philip six, Melanie just one, and Dean and I arrived in the capital to prepare to leave. I was inebriated with the kaleidoscope of color found in Asuncion. I had forgotten how vibrant green could be. No dust in the air. The trees all but "cried with color," as Edna St. Vincent Millay once said.

March 1977

We have one more month of summer left. I'm elated about it, but for the children it will be school once more, and they are not thrilled. Last week Melanie learned to balance on Christina's bicycle, just in time to practice riding it to Kindergarten.

This summer was not as uncomfortable as others I remember. Although often the temperatures soared well over a hundred degrees, it only lasted for a week or so before the cooling rains prevented it from becoming unbearable. The abundant rainfall transformed the drab Chaco into a beauty all its own. The main highway, still not paved, was closed weeks at a time. Vehicles en route to or from Asuncion were stuck. Shelves in the stores were getting bare, and many necessary items were unavailable.

Our mission stations became completely dependent on the airplane, which a year ago had three pilots, but since December only one. We see Dean very seldom these days. I'm sure that when our children look back on this period of their life, the most vivid picture of their dad will be of him sitting at the dining room table asleep over his log books.

With the return to the U.S. of our other pilot, our family has lost valuable friends as well as co-workers. Philip seems to feel it the keenest, as his friend Tommy is no longer here.

July 1978

From Dean:

There is never a dull moment in the life of a pilot on the mission field. It's not that my flying schedule has been less demanding, nor that the bookkeeping, maintenance on the airplane, breakdown of vehicles, or government-required paper work has lessened, but that there appears to be a lack of personnel here in Filadelfia, which made my work so diversified.

I just returned from a week's stay in Asuncion where I had flown missionaries to a mid-year conference. On the way down, as well as on the return, there were many stops to pick up people from different stations. On returning home, I became the chauffeur for two of our nurses who needed to be taken to the various Ayore camps to administer vaccinations.

Since we are negotiating for a piece of land for the Ayores and since none of the missionaries are in town, the job of transacting business concerning the negotiation is another one of my duties. I've only mentioned a few of the activities which keep me busy. However, this is only the beginning. The family who has been doing the buying, bookkeeping, and administration, has been asked to move to the capital to take over the print shop. This leaves our family with additional responsibilities which we can only assume through your intercessory prayers.

We are thrilled with the Ache people's response to the Gospel. After several years of working with them, recently 70 of them made decisions for Christ. Already the transformed life can be evidenced in their behavior.

April 1979

The most thrilling event this year was when the Totobiegosode were contacted in January. They are a small indigenous Ayore group for whom we have long been praying. Twenty-seven Ayore men from the El Faro mission station went looking for them again the day after Christmas. They had sighted their village from the airplane. Then they spent four difficult weeks trying to locate them in the dense thorn-infested forest. These two groups had been mortal enemies before members of the Ayore group at the mission station were saved. So you can imagine the fear and hostility of the Totobiegosode when they realized that they were surrounded by this group of men. It took a lot of persuasion on the part of these men before the others finally threw down their spears and arrows. Four days later they found the women and children who had fled to hide.

They are now at the mission station. These people need your prayers. They have so many taboos concerning what they may eat, that the ones who are not willing to break the taboos go hungry much of the time. They are also not immune to the diseases of the civilized people. Pray that they may accept the Good News of the Gospel that the other Ayores are sharing with them.

The Ayores have been given a piece of land near Filadelfia for a permanent settlement. This is an answer to prayer. Now comes the job of organizing the Ayores in the work of developing this land.

Both Melanie and Philip were in the hospital in January. The doctor diagnosed their illness as hepatitis. They lost much weight, but they are now on the mend.

April 1982

This year more than ever, we have realized that the Chaco is a place of extremes. After the worst draught we had experienced in ten years, it rained seven and a half inches in twelve hours, and this after a week of heavy rains. The water has penetrated many houses here in Filadelfia. It forced the inhabitants to move and converted some streets into rivers and the rest of them into, what Melanie calls, chocolate pudding. We are thankful that our cisterns are full and overflowing, although not so glad about our sunken-in cesspool.

Every night we are serenaded by choruses of frogs and toads and bitten by mosquitos, *polverines* (no seeums), and other varieties of insects.

Road travel outside our colony has come to a standstill which is evident by the empty shelves in the stores. Although we miss the fruits and vegetables, there are plenty of local products such as meat and dairy products.

Dean has enjoyed working on the airplane in the new hangar, which has been in use for quite some time. However, until recently, he had to haul water from home to the airport. Now the cistern is completed, and the time and energy spent on lining things up and supervising the Ayores, have been worthwhile: First, because two Ayores have been trained as bricklayers, and secondly, because the water is especially necessary now to wash the mud off the airplane.

Studies at the local Mennonite school for our two girls started March second. Christina is a junior and Melanie a fifth grader. Their German and Spanish are quite good now. They are keeping up with the rest of the local students. Philip is waiting for his correspondence course to arrive from the States. Meanwhile he is roughing it in the wilderness, working with a land clearing crew.

The following article was written by Dean and Margaret Lattin for the Paraguayan Field Paper called "The Land of the Guarani."

His Last Flight

A stationary front had brought rain to the Chaco. My last flight had been a week ago and I was impatiently waiting for the weather to clear. Several flights had been scheduled, people were waiting to return to their homes and families, but the front had brought all travel to a standstill. Finally, seven days later, the airstrip was dry enough for take-off. Asuncion had reported a high ceiling and no rain. As I slithered through the muddy streets of Filadelfia to preflight the plane, I congratulated myself on not having slipped into the mire as my pessimistic family had predicted. However, as I was turning into the airport, the inevitable happened. Picking up myself, the suitcase and the motor bike from the grime, I walked into the shop and called home for a change of clothes.

Several minutes later I saw my daughter approaching. Her bicycle was covered with mud, and her clothes were a chocolate color. I was suddenly overcome by laughter. Christina, however, could not quite see the humor.

We did get away that afternoon, dodging rain showers, flying low in places, wondering at times if we would have to turn around. Everyone breathed a prayer of thankfulness when the aircraft hit the Asuncion runway.

My intention was to return early the next morning, weather permitting; however, instead, I was now on my way to Bahia Negra, the home of Luís and Jacobo Barboza. They had come to the capital earlier to seek medical help for Jacobo.

This was not the first time that these two were my passengers. In 1970, I flew Luís and his family to the Ayore mission station. They were the first missionaries to be sent out from the Chamacoco church. Not too long ago the Chamacocos had a reputation of being fierce marauders terrorizing the more timid indigenous people. Now the family was on their way to help our missionaries proclaim the Good News to the Ayores whose notoriety until recently was like that of the Chamacocos.

I had made many flights to the Ayore station since then. Upon landing I was always met by the boisterous Ayore; in the background Luís and Gilda, with their three sons, shyly waited their turn to be greeted.

Recently, Luís, after having been with the Ayore for six years, expressed a longing to see his people again. Once more his family were my passengers as I flew them back to their home in Bahia Negra.

Glancing at Luís from time to time while maneuvering the plane through high build-ups, I felt with him the emptiness, the emotional drain, the dull aching sorrow as I was wondering what was going through his mind. Was it the feeling of futility, the memory of constant set-backs which he had experienced? Was he visualizing his garden vanishing under the flooded river? Was he imagining the hunger that awaited his family this winter? Or maybe he was thinking of the joyous face of Gilda when she told him she was expecting a baby and how that joy turned to sorrow when a few months ago she miscarried. Was it the burden of the Chamacoco church, which started so vivaciously but had lost its first love, that was lying heavily on his shoulders? Or was he recalling, as I had been, the wonder and excitement, the enthusiasm of his oldest son Jacobo through whose eyes he would never see his surroundings again?

I can still picture Jacobo sitting at our table, propped up on books, looking at his father with eyes wide with wonder, exclaiming: "It's ice daddy, it's ice!" "They call it ice cream here Jacobo," his father responded with a smile.

Our children were astonished that this boy, almost seven years old, was tasting ice cream for the first time. They were also pleased that this pleasant discovery should come to him at our home.

Luís and Jacobo had come to Filadelfia by tractor from the Ayore station on one of the mission's supply trips. There were several new experiences awaiting the seven year old as he proudly accompanied his dad to our small town that day.

Today was to be the last time that son and father were to travel together. The realization of this must be breaking the father's heart. He was probably wondering how he was to tell Gilda the news. She had such faith in her son's recovery when he and Jacobo left for Asuncion. Now she was to receive her first-born in a box.

As I was making my final approach, I confessed again my feeling of helplessness to the Lord and asked Him who alone is able to comfort the broken-hearted, to begin a work of healing in the souls of my friends.

"Jacobo, you who so much enjoyed flying with me, have flown for the last time. But never mind, you are experiencing joys you never dreamed of as you are looking into the face of the children's Friend."

Christina graduated from the local high school and went on to the New Tribes Mission School in Tambo, Bolivia, for one semester to improve her English skills. From there, she studied at Biola University in southern California, UCLA, and Pepperdine. She teaches American History to eighth graders. Philip studied mechanical engineering at Le Tourneau College. Melanie graduated from Biola College and home-schools her four daughters. Philip is working in Bolivia with NTM as government representative. Most of their education was paid for by friends of Martha, the Mennards.

Upon returning to the U.S. in 1990, Dean has flown as a survey pilot both in Burbank and Riverside, California.

.

Made in the USA
Middletown, DE
12 October 2022

12578135R00116